MW01277258

THE RISE OF VIRTUAL ASSISTANTS
How Hiring Virtual Assistants is Reshaping the Future of Business

All Rights Reserved

COPYRIGHT © 2023 Chris Kille

This book may not be reproduced, transmitted, or stored in whole or in part by any means, including graphic, electronic, or mechanical, without the express written consent of the publisher except in the case of brief questions embodied in critical articles and reviews.

ISBN: 979-8-9889044-0-3

Cover design: Jayson Caluag | jaysoncruzcaluag.com

Edited by Hilary Jastram | www.bookmarkpub.com

THE RISE OF VIRTUAL ASSISTANTS

CHRIS KILLE

GET IN TOUCH

For help hiring your own virtual assistant and to access your
free resource kit, visit ChrisKille.com/resources.

TABLE OF CONTENTS

INTRODUCTION

A few years back, I embarked on an experimental journey through the dynamic and productive world of virtual assistants (also known as VAs). I've always been fascinated by the idea of working remotely, and I was eager to learn more about how virtual assistants could help businesses succeed. Working with my first VA was actually more of an accidental circumstance. I'll tell you the story in the next chapter, so make sure to keep reading!

I quickly learned that virtual assistants offer a whole new level of flexibility and convenience. They can provide specialized skills and expertise without the typical headaches associated with traditional employment—meaning businesses can save money on office space, equipment, and benefits while gaining access to a global pool of talent.

FINDING VIRTUAL ASSISTANTS

The Philippines is one of the leading countries in the virtual assistant industry. Its highly skilled and English-proficient workforce, combined with strong government support for remote work initiatives, has made it a popular destination for businesses seeking virtual support.

English is widely spoken and understood there, making it easier for virtual assistants to communicate effectively with clients from English-speaking countries. The Philippines also has a strong educational system emphasizing English language proficiency. Because many Filipinos are fluent in English, this is a significant advantage for virtual assistants as they can seamlessly handle tasks such as customer support, content creation, administrative work, and more.

I'm excited to continue my journey into the world of virtual assistants, and I believe this industry has the potential to revolutionize the way businesses operate. I'm already a part of it.

I've learned these facts about virtual assistants:

- They can provide a wide range of services, including administrative, creative, and technical task support.

- Businesses save time and money and improve their productivity when using virtual assistants.

- You can access virtual assistants worldwide, which gives you and your business the flexibility to hire the best talent, regardless of location.

- Virtual assistants are a valuable asset to businesses of all sizes.

If you're a business owner or entrepreneur, I encourage you to learn more about virtual assistants. They could be the key to helping you take your business to the next level. I am a shining example of how you can reap the fruits of their labor while maximizing your time.

WHAT IS A VIRTUAL ASSISTANT?

I've been a business owner for over twenty years and have learned a lot about what it takes to be successful. ***One of the most important lessons you can learn is figuring out you can't do everything yourself.*** You need to delegate tasks to others to free up your time so you can focus on the things that only you can do.

That's where virtual assistants come in. These wonderful people are remote workers who can help you with a variety of responsibilities in the following various areas:

- Administrative: Handling data entry, calendar management, organizing and responding to emails, and so on.

- Creative: Writing or creating content in some form, like blogs, scripts, videos, documents, etc., and performing other related tasks, such as managing social media platforms, conducting research, running email campaigns, etc.

- Technical: Website design and development, graphic design, and video editing, for starters.

Hiring a virtual assistant is a smart way to save time and money, and it can help you improve your business's efficiency and productivity.

I have discovered these specific benefits from hiring virtual assistants:

- **Saving Time**: Virtual assistants can help you to free up your time so you can focus on your core responsibilities. They give you more time to spend on strategic planning, networking, and growing your business.

- **Saving Money**: Virtual assistants are typically less expensive than hiring full-time employees. You don't pay for office space, benefits, or training.

- **Improving Efficiency**: Your decreased workload means you can work faster with fewer errors.

- **Boosting Productivity**: Virtual assistants improve your business's productivity by working on tasks you may not have the time or expertise to handle. You will accomplish more and achieve your business goals faster.

If you're considering hiring a virtual assistant, there are a few things you should keep in mind to cultivate the most successful relationship possible:

- **Define Your Needs**: Before you start looking for a virtual assistant, it's important to define your needs. What tasks do you need help with? What skills and experience are you looking for?

3

- **Do Your Research**: There are many virtual assistants out there, so it's important to do your research and find one who is a good fit. Read reviews, check references, and interview potential candidates before hiring.

- **Set Clear Expectations**: Once you've hired a virtual assistant, set clear expectations. What tasks do you expect them to complete? What are your deadlines? How often will you communicate?

- **Provide Feedback**: Give feedback on a regular basis to help your VA improve their performance and ensure they are meeting your expectations.

TAKING A STEP FORWARD

Hiring a virtual assistant is a strategic way to improve your business's efficiency, productivity, and profitability. If you're looking for a way to save time and money and get more done, I'm telling you, this is it.

Working together, whether in person or virtually, is the key to achieving success. Virtual assistants offer a unique opportunity to enhance collaboration, streamline processes, and achieve business objectives more effectively.

My virtual assistants are powerhouses and as important to include in my business strategy as software programs or organizational platforms that push me to work smarter, not harder. They utilize artificial intelligence, machine learning, and natural language processing to interact with users and perform assigned tasks quickly and accurately. The right assistants can handle a wide range of activities, as I mentioned, and when you combine this strength with their use of technology, it feels like they are virtually unstoppable.

One of the primary advantages of hiring a virtual assistant is improved efficiency. When they are at the wheel, you can dedicate your energy to strategic decision-making, creativity, and value-added tasks that contribute directly to your business growth.

WHY AM I SO PASSIONATE ABOUT VIRTUAL ASSISTANTS?

Before I go any further, let me share the amazing adventures I've had with virtual assistants, specifically those from the Philippines. From the positive impacts to the occasional setbacks, I'll let you know everything I went through, so you can have the best experience possible when you hire your own virtual assistant.

My journey began unintentionally. One day, I discovered I'd scaled my business to the point where I could no longer do it alone. I wanted to continue expanding and be more prosperous, but if I was going to do that, I needed help.

So, I went on the hunt . . . and I learned a lot.

In trying to find just the right person to help me, I encountered more and more business assistants abroad. And in the midst of this undertaking, an unexpected sense of purpose took root. I could see the benefit of both giving and receiving help. I was about to take part in transforming lives overseas, in contributing to the industry boom by working with some of the most proficient and polite people I had ever met. Years on, it's something I'm still incredibly proud of.

Helping in this way wasn't my original intention (although I certainly wasn't opposed to the idea!). Now, I've found immense fulfillment in making a positive impact on people's lives.

Navigating the Competitive Credit Card Processing Industry

Within the cutthroat credit card processing industry, I sought an edge to allow the company to grow consistently beyond a one-man show. At a conference in Charleston, South Carolina, I stumbled upon a speaker who ran a successful virtual assistant company based in the Philippines. I was intrigued by his setup and satisfied clients and explored the possibility of using their services. But when I saw the pricing and only a few stimulating reviews, I decided to chart my own course.

SOLO ADVENTURES IN HIRING VIRTUAL ASSISTANTS

I couldn't shake the feeling that I was onto a new and smarter way of doing business as I did my own work to find virtual assistants. I scoured online job boards, such as onlinejobs.ph. These became my treasure trove. I dove headfirst into posting positions for customer service, personal assistance, social media management, graphic design, and web design. But the process was difficult and time-consuming. Sorting through a flood of applicants, many of whom were unqualified, required significant effort and strained my productivity. Trying to vet people turned into resume review marathons and became a full-time job.

After reviewing and enduring countless resumes and interviews, I hired Dee. Since I am all about honesty, I will tell you that she was just okay, but she was very friendly. A winning personality is not going to get the job done. After a brief spin around the block with her, back to the drawing board, I went. I share this also because it's important to understand that you might not get the right fit with your first choice. Keep trying until you find the person who suits your team. It took me a few tries, and I am glad I kept at it.

Next, I hired Claudia, who, shortly after signing, moved to Australia to be with her partner (I don't blame her!). There were a couple of others with a more generalized skill set—but that wasn't going to work for me. Once I figured out that I needed a person with more advanced skills and I onboarded him, it changed everything. I could breathe.

The goal is to shorten your hiring process and get the optimal candidate. I know this. Keep in mind I was brand-new to this task. It took me a minute. That's why I wrote this book and started my company; I wanted to give you the experience I didn't have and help you find exactly who you are looking for.

Throughout the process of onboarding people, I was thrust into a brand-new learning curve as I navigated granting access to my sensitive information. The absence of password management software meant my virtual assistants had access to everything from bank accounts to social media—this was definitely a leap of faith on my part, and I wasn't entirely comfortable with it. Now, I use password management software to maintain my security (and I suggest you do, too!).

Yes, I was building the plane while trying to fly it! I didn't have any Key Performance Indicators (KPIs) or Standard Operating Procedures (SOPs), so I had to repeatedly teach everything my jobs entailed, resulting in a significant waste of time. Eventually, I realized that I needed to create KPIs and SOPs to streamline performance.

If you don't know, KPIs are measurable goals that help you track your virtual assistant's performance (or any performance). For example, you might set a KPI for your VA to complete a certain number of tasks per day or week. SOPs are step-by-step instructions that outline how tasks should be completed. An SOP could outline how to create a new blog post or respond to customer inquiries.

Once I created KPIs and SOPs, it was much easier to manage my virtual assistant's performance. I could easily track progress and identify areas needing improvement. I could also provide feedback and training as needed. As a result, performance improved significantly.

In addition to KPIs and SOPs, I implemented a few other changes that helped to improve his performance. I started using project management software to track work and assign tasks. I also incorporated video conferencing to communicate with my VA on a regular basis. These changes improved communication and collaboration, leading to even better results.

When my present VA was fully trained and comfortable with my expectations, suddenly, my workload lightened. This only increased when I next handed over the job of recruiting customer service representatives. With that out of the way, I could focus more on selling—my preferred role.

I could also concentrate on activities that generated more revenue instead of being consumed by time-sucking tasks. It took my present VA and me over a year to establish a solid working relationship. Eventually, he became proficient enough to perform tasks without constantly seeking guidance.

That was a game-changer.

CREATING A TEAM

With the hiring of a team came significant business growth, equaling more customers and increased revenue. I realized the value of affordable Filipino assistants handling administrative tasks and shared this discovery with friends. I then helped them find suitable virtual assistants for their businesses, which led to successful collaborations.

As I continued learning about the process, I attended a conference where I gained insights from professionals who specialized in this field. That's when I learned there was a broader market beyond entry-level roles, including individuals with extensive management experience from various companies worldwide. This potential excited me so much that I spent six months building an infrastructure to launch my own VA business before taking on clients, so I could ensure a solid foundation for success.

However, as is often the case when creating something new, I made some mistakes along the way. As I focused on sales and acquiring new clients, I neglected the day-to-day management of my team, resulting in a shift in company culture and a negative work environment. A costly investment in a building facilitated an undesirable atmosphere as well. To address these issues, I had to make the difficult decision to let go of most of the team and rebuild.

With the knowledge of what not to do fresh in my mind, I implemented a more effective hiring and management process. Bringing in experienced professionals, establishing clear roles and responsibilities, and implementing KPIs and accountability measures, created a stronger and more productive company culture. Although there is still some rebuilding to do, I am confident in the direction we are heading.

This journey taught me valuable lessons about management, culture, and the importance of learning from both successes and failures. As I reshape my company, I now have the opportunity to leverage my expertise to assist others in achieving their goals—and I have great assistants right beside me. There's nothing more rewarding than helping others minimize their growing pains with my experience.

MOVING ON

Now that I have been working in the virtual assistant industry for several years, I have become incredibly passionate about the transformative potential of it. While the concept of remote work has been around for some time, the rise of virtual assistants has opened up new opportunities for businesses and professionals looking to achieve more with less.

There are several reasons why I am so passionate about virtual assistants.

First, I believe that virtual assistants offer a powerful solution to one of the biggest challenges facing modern businesses: staying agile and competitive in an ever-changing landscape. By leveraging the skills and expertise of remote professionals, businesses can achieve a level of flexibility and scalability that would be impossible with traditional in-house hiring models. This allows them to pivot quickly in response to changing market conditions without being tied down by overheads and administrative burdens.

Second, I love virtual assistants because of the economic and social benefits they provide. As someone who is passionate about creating opportunities for others, I believe that the growth of the virtual assistant industry in the Philippines and other developing countries has the potential to transform the lives of millions of people. By providing employment opportunities to skilled virtual assistants who may not have access to traditional job markets, we enable them to help drive economic growth and reduce inequality.

Third, virtual assistants offer unique opportunities to professionals looking to build flexible and fulfilling careers. As someone who has always valued freedom and flexibility, I believe the rise of virtual assistants has created a new model for work that allows professionals to achieve a better work-life balance while still pursuing their passions and goals. Virtual assistants are on the winning end of this equation, too. They can leverage their skills and expertise to build a career on their own terms without being tied down by traditional employment models.

Finally, I am a fervent fan of virtual assistants because of the impact they have on the world. As someone who is committed to creating positive change, I believe virtual assistants offer powerful solutions to some of the biggest challenges we face, from climate change to poverty to inequality. Applying the skills and expertise of a global network of remote professionals means even smaller businesses can contribute to a more sustainable and equitable world.

I love virtual assistants because they can perform amazing tasks to help make our lives better.

Sure, there might be some challenges when you first onboard your VA, like figuring out how to manage someone or even a team of people who work overseas, but the good they can do outweighs any problems. I truly believe that virtual assistants can change the world for the better by revolutionizing how we work and making positive ripples all around us!

What you can expect to learn from this book . . . .

I wrote this book for you to gain a deeper understanding of the concept of virtual assistants and their transformative potential for businesses and individuals alike.

Here's a brief overview of the coming pages:

- **Chapter 1**: Why virtual assistants are beneficial for businesses and individuals and the support they provide in areas like administration, technical services, sales, marketing, social media, content creation, research, and personal assistance.

- **Chapter 2**: An explanation of the different industries and professions that benefit from using virtual assistants and the specific tasks and projects they handle to make business operations more efficient.

- **Chapter 3**: The benefits of using a virtual assistant, including cost-effectiveness, access to a skilled workforce, language proficiency, time zone advantages, cultural compatibility, strong work ethics, flexibility, scalability, and a core competency focus.

- **Chapter 4**: The advantages and unique challenges of using a virtual assistant like communication difficulties, time zone differences, maintaining work quality, ensuring confidentiality, building reliability and competency, and considering infrastructure requirements.

- **Chapter 5**: A deep dive into why Filipino virtual assistants have gained popularity recently and the factors contributing to the increasing demand for their services, including an explanation of Filipino culture and how it has become a prominent hub for virtual assistants.

- **Chapter 6**: A debunking of the common misunderstandings about virtual assistants and straightforward explanations to help businesses understand what to expect when working with them.

- **Chapter 7**: How to make the most of virtual assistants—including the implementation of effective processes, practical advice for managing virtual assistants, and integrating them into your business operations.

CHAPTER 1

Why Use a VA?

"Don't sweat the small things. Pay for services as if you are a $10M company, especially if it saves you time or speeds you up."
—Darius Cheung

As a business owner, I am no stranger to the perils and pitfalls of managing a growing company. There's always so much to do, and it can be overwhelming to handle everything on your own. That's where virtual assistants come in.

Virtual assistants are skilled professionals who can help with a wide range of tasks remotely. They can take care of things like managing your schedule and dealing with customer inquiries, freeing up your time and energy. In this chapter, I'll share some of the ways that virtual assistants have helped my business grow.

TIME MANAGEMENT

One of the best things about working with a virtual assistant is how they can help you manage your time more effectively. I know firsthand how overwhelming it can be to have a never-ending to-do list. But here's the thing: Not all of those tasks require your personal attention. Your new VA can step in and make a real difference.

Remember my experience that made me realize the power of working with a VA?

When my business started growing rapidly, I found myself drowning in administrative tasks. All day long, I was engaged in the onboarding of new customers, customer service tasks, providing technical support, and managing compliance-related to-dos, all while handling the daily operations of running a business. I literally had no other time to dedicate to anything else. My day was spent putting out fires and being more reactive than proactive. This relentless workload was incredibly draining. As I sit here and write this book, I remember being so frustrated and overwhelmed; I didn't know what my next step should be.

After fighting myself enough, I decided to hire a VA. And when I did, I was amazed at how much weight came off my shoulders. My VA took over tasks like scheduling appointments, managing my inbox, and organizing files. Suddenly, I had more time to devote to strategic planning, making critical decisions, and taking care of my clients.

But it didn't stop there. My VA also proved invaluable in helping with social media management and content creation. He brought fresh ideas and expertise to our marketing efforts, helping us connect with our audience in more meaningful ways. With his support, our online presence grew stronger, so we could reach more potential customers.

My present VA is incredibly thoughtful and proactive. I suspect he considers how he can help me with any task I assign. He will suggest ways to structure processes and is anticipatory, completing jobs I haven't even asked him to do. He sees what I am trying to accomplish as he supports and improves my best efforts. Before I found him, I didn't understand the full scope of what a VA could do.

Our relationship is built on trust, and this is what I want you to understand. I have to step back and demonstrate that I believe he is capable; I have to allow an environment for learning and making mistakes we will grow from. I did note that the more I tried to tell him how to do something, it didn't work. Everything runs much more smoothly when I stay in my lane.

Make sure you are cultivating trust with your VA, so both of you will get the most out of your relationship.

And when I say that a VA can make a real difference in managing your time, I truly mean it. I am living it. And I am such a raving fan; I built a whole business around it. Virtual assistants take on those time-consuming tasks, allowing you to focus on what truly matters for your business and giving you the freedom to thrive and take your business to new heights.

COST EFFICIENCY

Let me tell you a little story that perfectly illustrates how working with a virtual assistant can be a game-changer in terms of cost savings. When I first started my own business, I was on a tight budget. Every penny counted, and I had to find a way to get the help I needed without breaking the bank. Business went on like that for a while—until I couldn't take it anymore.

When I hit a growth milestone, I discovered the power of working with a VA. Not only did they provide the support I needed, they offered a cost-effective solution that positively impacted my business finances.

Here's how it played out.

I was considering hiring an in-house employee to handle some administrative tasks and support me in day-to-day operations. But as I looked into it further, I realized the financial implications were more significant than I initially thought. I would need to provide them with a physical workspace, furnish it with equipment, and take care of additional costs like health insurance and paid time off. It all added up and would be a huge burden for my growing business.

That's when I realized that by collaborating with a virtual assistant, I could bypass all those hefty overhead costs. Virtual assistants often work remotely, which meant I didn't need to find them a workspace or provide equipment. They had their own setup—such a huge relief for me.

The more I learned, the better it got. Working with a VA on a contract or freelance basis meant I would only pay for the specific services I needed. I didn't have to commit to a full-time employee with all the associated expenses. It was like having a talented professional on demand, available to support me 24/7.

I felt like I'd just uncovered one of the secrets of the universe. This arrangement is incredibly affordable if you'd rather have someone working exclusively for you, too. And if you don't need a VA as often or only need them for specific projects, no worries there, either! You can hire them full-time, part-time, or on a case-by-case basis. You design the arrangement according to your needs.

Check out some of the benefits of hiring a virtual assistant part-time:

- You can save money on salary and benefits.

- You'll have more flexible hours.

- There is a wider pool of candidates to choose from.

Ready to go all in? These are some of the benefits of hiring a virtual assistant full-time:

- A dedicated team member is always available to help you.

- You'll build a closer relationship with your virtual assistant.

- You have more control over the tasks that your virtual assistant completes.

As you can imagine, the best way to hire a virtual assistant is to decide what is best for your business and your needs. If you need someone available to help you 24/7, then hiring a full-time virtual assistant may be the best option for you. If you only need help during certain hours of the day, then hiring a part-time virtual assistant is probably the better choice.

Working with a VA turned out to be a cost-effective solution that made a world of difference for my business. It allowed me to get the support I needed without straining my budget. Plus, it gave me peace of mind knowing that I had a skilled professional by my side, ready to help whenever I needed them.

If you're in a similar situation and you need reliable and budget-conscious support, I highly recommend considering a VA. They can be a financial lifesaver as you scale.

In one instance that made me realize I could never go back to working the way I used to, I had a project that required intensive attention and support for a specific period. Hiring a full-time employee was overkill, and I didn't want to commit to a long-term arrangement. But working with a VA was perfect. The flexibility was unlike anything I'd experienced with other assistants.

Unlike traditional employees who work set hours, virtual assistants move and flex to the demands of your business. This meant I could bring in a VA for the exact number of hours or days required and that I wouldn't have any unnecessary overhead.

I also loved how my pool of candidates exploded since I wasn't limited to searching local talent only. No, I could work with anyone anywhere in the world. It's pretty mind-blowing if you think about it.

These professionals, now at my fingertips, brought unique perspectives and experiences. Suddenly, I had a global team at my fingertips.

Then there was the time zone advantage! I didn't realize how much of a difference it makes to give my clients round-the-clock support.

Imagine waking up in the morning to find that tasks and projects are progressing or have been completed while you slept! It was like having a dedicated team working tirelessly to ensure my business was always moving forward. Or maybe like a crew of elves that lived in my office that did the work while I wasn't looking!

Just like that, I had newfound flexibility. I could scale my business and easily adjust the level of support I required as my needs evolved. This was the solution I didn't even know existed!

ACCESS TO SPECIALIZED SKILLS

One of the many wonderful advantages of working with a virtual assistant is the ability to access a wealth of specialized skills and expertise. So, please make sure your VA has a diverse professional background. When you find the right person, it's less like working with a partner and more like forming a partnership with a person possessing extensive experience across many fields.

For example, if you're seeking assistance in bookkeeping, you can put the word out, and bam! Now you have a VA specializing in accounting. Or maybe you need graphic design work for your website. With the right VA, your project will be done in no time. Harnessing the specialized knowledge and skills of a VA enables you to beef up your workforce with the best candidates out there. Have you ever put on a suit tailored just for you? It's like that but for your business.

INCREASED PRODUCTIVITY

If you're like literally every businessperson out there, you can relate to needing to do more in a shorter period of time—and do it well. Your VA lets you reclaim your precious time and mental energy, allowing you to turbocharge your productivity and zero in on what truly matters—your goals and roles that move the needle in your business.

I'm not intimidated by taking on anything I've never done before. But I think differently now. Delegation first. Let your VA handle the jobs that take you a while but that they have done a thousand times.

And who has time for task prioritization? I know I don't. I can sit there and stare at my to-do list and get confused about what to tackle first. It seems like everything is a first priority! Virtual assistants perform the most important and urgent tasks before anything else, so you don't have to worry about getting them done. And you will streamline your workflow, kick stress to the curb, and push your overall productivity.

BUSINESS GROWTH SUPPORT

As you scale your business, the weight of responsibilities and the de-mands on your time can be overwhelming. Did you know not every task requires your personal touch? Don't worry! I didn't know that right away, either. I spent a good chunk of time overthinking, micro-managing, and obsessing. I was running in a circle. I don't want that to be your reality, so make a different choice. Don't take the long-cut like I did.

Your virtual assistant can act as your time management master. Entrust them with the tasks you don't want to do or shouldn't be doing (if they are more admin in nature) and reclaim working *on* your business, not *in* your business.

Take your all-consuming responsibilities off your plate, and your vir-tual assistant will give you back the best gift of all—time. Get ready to be proactive, not reactive. You're not a firefighter, so stop putting out those fires!

With the support of your virtual assistant, your business can oper-ate without a hitch as it thrives. After a time and investing in proper training (we'll get to that), your VA will become an integral part of your business. You can think of them as an extension of your talents. Together, you will realize an atmosphere of productivity, balance, and success.

Are you starting to see the big picture? Your business can thrive, your time can be returned, and you can have the freedom to enjoy life be-yond work. It's all within reach.

GLOBAL REACH

We talked about the benefit of picking from the best candidates in the *world*. Consider this: Your VA's global reach gives your business a competitive edge. They are worldly, used to communicating with other cultures, and Filipino professionals, especially, have been brought up to be incredibly solicitous.

This trait in your VA becomes especially valuable if you have an international business or serve clients from diverse cultural backgrounds. Your virtual assistant is your trusted cultural guide, helping you navigate nuances in various societies and ensuring that your business is equipped to cater to your clients' unique needs.

Not only does this new face of your company invite people in with their expansive communication skills, it doesn't matter the time of day a client reaches out to you. Because you are leveraging 24/7 support and representation. That only improves your reputation—a goal that can't be overstated.

IMPROVED WORK-LIFE BALANCE

Running a business is time-consuming, and it can be challenging to find time for personal and family commitments. A virtual assistant can alleviate some of the pressure, so you can live a more balanced lifestyle. Delegate tasks to your virtual assistant so that outside of the office, you have time for what matters most: family and friends.

This next point is one of my favorites. As a slammed entrepreneur or business owner, you are at risk of burnout. Maybe you've already felt those signs? Enter your brand-new virtual assistant. Yes, they will also help you reduce the risk of burnout and can decrease your stress. And you know you have to take care of your mental or physical health, or there won't be a business to run! Although it's demanding to do what you do, you can do it differently. You can delegate tasks to your virtual assistant (you really can, I promise!), avoid overworking yourself, and stay dialed into responsibilities that add the most value.

People just like you and me with smaller businesses can now access the secret of monster corporations. No longer is it just the C-suite executives who seem like they have eight arms and have cloned themselves, taking advantage of remote work arrangements. Virtual assistants provide valuable support to businesses of all sizes and industries.

Stop fighting it already. There's no reason you can't access what so many other executives are doing.

In the next chapter, we'll explore the various skills and services virtual assistants offer, so you can you find the right fit for your business.

Let me help you take that first step. Reach out to chriskille.com/resources to learn more.

CHAPTER 2

What Can a VA Do For You?

"The secret to getting ahead is getting started."
—Mark Twain

The title of this chapter is pretty self-explanatory, so let's dive into it! These are all the things a VA can do for you that you might not even know about. Some people get the "assistant" part of the phrase confused. They think it means a VA can only do admin tasks. But this role involves far more than just admin-oriented tasks: Virtual assistants can plan your events, manage travel, even execute specialized tasks, and so on. Keep reading because I am about to blow your mind with the potential awaiting you and your business.

ADMINISTRATIVE SUPPORT

Virtual assistants are capable of providing various administrative support *and other* services to businesses and entrepreneurs. Understanding how to use and leverage technology, for instance, is vital to your business. In this section, I will go over all the admin duties you can assign to your VA. In later sections, we will cover different assignments outside of the admin designation, like technology.

- **Appointment Scheduling:** Virtual assistants can manage the calendar of a business owner or executive. They can schedule meetings, appointments, and reminders. Now, you can stay on top of your schedule and avoid double-booking or missing appointments.

- **Customer Support**: Virtual assistants can handle customer inquiries, complaints, and support tickets. They can provide customers with quick and efficient solutions to their problems, improving your customer experience.

- **Social Media Management**: Social media is a critical component of any business's marketing strategy. A virtual assistant can manage a company's social media accounts, create content, and engage with followers. If you don't have time to reply to every little comment, your worries are over. Your VA can help your business increase its social media presence and even attract more customers.

- **Data Entry**: Data entry is a time-consuming and repetitive task that can be outsourced to a virtual assistant. If you are an executive and doing this, stop it! A virtual assistant can enter data into spreadsheets, databases, and other software, so you don't have to do it.

- **Bookkeeping**: Virtual assistants can help with bookkeeping tasks such as invoicing, bill payment, and account reconciliation. Train them properly to meet your business needs, and your finances will be accurate and up to date.

- **Research:** Use a virtual assistant to conduct research on a variety of topics, such as industry trends, what your competitor is up to, and identifying and locating potential clients. Research allows businesses to make informed decisions and stay ahead of the competition.

- **Travel Arrangements**: For as long as executive assistants have been around, they have made travel arrangements. Now, you can enjoy that luxury. Virtual assistants can make travel arrangements for business owners and executives, such as booking flights, hotels, and rental cars. Wouldn't it be nice if all your travel plans were well-organized and stress-free?

- **Email Management:** One of the primary tasks of a virtual assistant is to manage emails, including sorting and categorizing them and responding promptly to any urgent messages.

Before I hired my VA, my inbox was a labyrinth of unanswered messages, urgent requests, and endless subscriptions. It was a constant battle to stay on top of it all and maintain timely communication with clients and partners.

One day, I'd had it. It felt like all I'd done was gotten lost in email hell for ten hours. So, I enlisted the help of a virtual assistant from the Philippines to take over this and other responsibilities.

After I trained them for a few short days, I regained control.

Virtual assistants bring their expertise and dedication and not only alleviate your burdens, but they do it with a sense of calm and order. Now, you can finally enjoy more productivity and peace of mind.

Take it from someone who has walked this path. Give yourself this gift. Embrace the support of a virtual assistant managing your inbox. Experience the transformation I lived firsthand and discover the freedom awaiting you.

In case you are reading and thinking, *Chris, I could never let anyone handle my personal business—my emails contain very sensitive information!* I hear you. I had that opinion, too. Let me tell you what you can do to keep yourself and other people safe.

TRUST AND BOUNDARIES IN COMMUNICATION

You must establish trust and boundaries with your VA when they are responding to your emails. Before you allow them access, provide them with a list of approved senders and topics, and let them know when you are unavailable to respond to emails. Have a system in place for approving VA-generated responses before they are sent out, and make sure expectations are clear surrounding your email rules. Use the information below to develop the standards and protocols that will work for you.

Standards and Protocols

There are a number of standards and protocols that should be in place when a VA is responding to emails on behalf of a business owner or executive. These standards and protocols should ensure that the VA is responding in a professional and timely manner and that they are not disclosing any confidential or sensitive information.

Here is an example of a standard and protocol:

- All emails must be approved by the business owner or executive before they are sent out.

- The VA must not disclose any confidential/sensitive information to any recipients. If there is a question as to how an email should be replied to, the VA needs to seek approval before sending a response.

- The VA must respond to emails within twenty-four hours of receiving them.

Establishing trust and boundaries, and putting standards and protocols in place, gives all parties the appropriate expectations and governs your VA's conduct in this area. Now, you can feel assured that your VA is responding to your emails in a professional and safe manner.

With that concern out of the way, let's get a little more granular about the specific email tasks they can perform:

- **Sorting and Filtering Emails**: As I mentioned, a virtual assistant can sort and filter emails based on their priority, sender, and content. When in the world would you have time to do this? Important emails are addressed on the spot, while less important ones can be dealt with later or even deleted.

- **Responding to Emails:** A VA can respond to emails on behalf of a business owner or executive. They can draft responses, seek approval, and send messages out in a timely manner.

- **Organizing Emails:** They can be tasked to organize emails into specific folders or categories, such as by project, client, or topic. This makes it easier to find emails when needed and ensures that important information is not lost or overlooked.

- **Unsubscribing from Mailing Lists**: A virtual assistant can unsubscribe from unwanted mailing lists and spam emails, reducing clutter in your inbox and improving email management. If I never have to hit the unsubscribe button again, that would be okay with me!

- **Setting up Email Templates**: Virtual assistants can set up email templates for frequently sent emails, such as thank you notes or responses to common questions. Now, you're saving time and keeping your emails consistent and professional.

- **Scheduling Email Reminders**: A virtual assistant can schedule reminders for follow-up emails, deadlines, or meetings. No longer will you forget important tasks or where you have to be.

Let's move on to some other tasks you will definitely want to delegate.

Calendar Management

- **Scheduling/Rescheduling Appointments**: A virtual assistant can schedule and reschedule appointments, manage your calendar, suggest available times, and send out invitations to attendees. Appointments are organized and attended on time. This task, in my opinion, is one of the heaviest time-consuming distractions we fight.

- **Managing Meeting Invitations**: A virtual assistant can manage meeting invitations, RSVPs, and attendee lists. They can send out reminders and confirmations and ensure all attendees are prepared for the meeting.

- **Setting Reminders and Notifications:** This is yet another job that chips away at your time. Your VA can set up reminders and notifications for upcoming appointments, meetings, or deadlines. Important tasks now stay top-of-mind.

- **Blocking Time for Focus:** If you're not using this trick, you need to. A virtual assistant can block out time on your calendar for focus and productivity. You're no longer scrambling to find time to strategize your business. You can actually use the time to implement tactics for growth.

- **Coordinating Team Meetings:** A virtual assistant can also coordinate team meetings, such as weekly check-ins or status updates. They can manage the calendar, invite attendees, and prepare an agenda so no one is wasting their time wondering what the hell the meeting is about.

Travel Management

Travel planning can be a daunting task, especially if you have a busy schedule. Virtual assistants can make your travel arrangements and book flights, hotels, and car rentals. They can keep track of your travel itineraries, so you can stay organized throughout your trip.

A couple of years ago, I was swamped and had an upcoming cross-country business trip that seemed destined for chaos. Meetings were piling up, a crucial deadline loomed overhead, and I had a laundry list of travel arrangements to handle. It was a perfect storm of compounding tasks, and it left me completely overwhelmed.

Thank goodness, once again, for my VA's remarkable gift for time management. She understood the significance of my trip and my limited time, and she dove right in. She actually seemed to love these tasks. That makes one of us! She guided me through all the travel planning, and I never missed a beat or a flight—because she never did. That is the amazing thing about virtual assistants—when you pick the right one through a legitimate VA hiring channel, they can save your you-know-what.

My VA researched the best flight options that made the most sense with my preferences and demanding schedule. She effortlessly coordinated time zones, connecting flights, and airport logistics, and when she was done, presented me with a flawless itinerary. Somehow, she even minimized my travel time. I swear, it was magic!

Next, my VA turned her attention to finding the ideal hotel accommodations. She knew I needed a place where I would feel comfortable enough to work, so she spent a little extra time here. I let her do her thing, and she didn't disappoint as she meticulously vetted options, considering factors like my proximity to meeting locations and amenities that made my stay feel as close to home as possible. My hotel exceeded my expectations in every way.

Once she was done with that, my VA curated a comprehensive travel itinerary that left no detail to chance. Flights, hotel reservations, meeting schedules, transportation arrangements—everything I needed to know about was documented and easily accessible. Her attention kept me on top of my game, so I could crush it at my meetings.

I was so thankful for how smoothly everything fell into place. She had anticipated my every need. Thanks to her exceptional time management skills, my trip was awesome—it even surpassed all my expectations—and that's hard to do! Maybe I was just used to flying by the seat of my pants, frantically searching for details, and rushing through airports so I wouldn't miss my flights. If I had done it my way, I would have, most likely, missed two or three very important client meetings, resulting in potential lost revenue.

It wasn't just that she was so skillful in handling these details. How she handled it was a red light to me that I *shouldn't* be doing some jobs in my business. Now, every trip I take is stress-free; I can show up as my best self and make the most of every opportunity in front of me.

Whether you're a seasoned traveler or getting ready to take your first trip, I highly encourage you to embrace having your virtual assistant manage your travel. Don't you think you deserve the peace of mind that comes from having such a skilled time-management guru? I do.

Here's a breakdown of what a VA can do for you in travel management.

- **Booking Flights and Hotels**: A virtual assistant can research and book flights and hotels for employees; they can consider their preferences, schedules, and budgets as they monitor prices and make itinerary adjustments.

- **Arranging Transportation**: Put down your phone! You don't need to coordinate transportation to and from airports, hotels, and other destinations anymore. Your VA can book rental cars, taxis, or ride-sharing services. Once you arrive at your destination, they can communicate with local transportation providers to ensure you have safe and reliable transportation options.

- **Managing Itineraries**: A virtual assistant can create detailed itineraries for employees, including flight and hotel information, transportation arrangements, meeting schedules, and other important details. They can also send reminders and notifications to ensure that employees are on time and prepared.

- **Coordinating Meals and Entertainment**: Dining on the road can be a pain. A virtual assistant can coordinate meals and entertainment for you, including making restaurant reservations, ordering room service, or arranging for catering at meetings or events.

- **Handling Travel Emergencies**: You've got a partner when things go sideways now. Your VA can be your go-to if you have a travel emergency, such as a flight cancellation, lost luggage, or medical emergencies. They can quickly make alternate travel arrangements to keep you safe.

- **Managing Travel Expenses**: Returning home always brings with it a wallet full of receipts. A virtual assistant can manage travel expenses, ensuring that receipts are collected, expenses are recorded accurately, and reimbursements are processed in a timely manner.

- **Researching Local Information**: I call this part of traveling "the catch-all," as it covers everything else involved in traveling, like researching information, such as local customs, weather conditions, and safety tips. If you're at a loss for what to eat or what sites to see, your VA can provide recommendations for restaurants, attractions, and other activities to make your trip memorable.

Data Entry

Data entry is a repetitive task requiring accuracy and attention to detail. Virtual assistants can assist with data entry tasks, so your business data is up-to-date and accurate. This itemized list provides more information.

- **Data Collection:** Data collection from different sources, such as paper documents, digital files, or online platforms, can overwhelm you. Let a VA take charge here. They can extract relevant information and organize it in a structured manner for further use.

- **Data Formatting:** Some data requires a little more attention. Your VA can create tables, adjust fonts, or apply consistent styling. It's paramount that your data is presented uniformly and is easy to interpret.

- **Data Transcription:** If you've got audio or video recordings needing transcribing, this is another job for your virtual assistant. It's particularly useful for businesses that conduct interviews, meetings, or conferences and need accurate and organized records of the spoken content.

- **Database Management:** Virtual assistants can input data into databases, update existing records, or ensure data integrity. They can also assist in creating and maintaining a well-organized database structure.

- **Data Cleaning:** Data is an ongoing job—that you don't have to deal with anymore. Virtual assistants can clean and validate data by removing duplicate entries, correcting errors, or standardizing information. This improves data quality and minimizes inaccuracies or inconsistencies within the dataset.

- **Spreadsheet Management:** Spreadsheet management is not a problem for your virtual assistant. They can enter data into pre-defined templates, write formulas, and generate reports based on data. Your business can now organize and analyze information effectively.

- **Data Migration:** When businesses transition to new systems or merge databases, a virtual assistant can assist in migrating data by transferring and organizing information from one platform to another. No more lost data or stumbling over new processes while trying to work with the old.

- **Online Data Entry:** This is another niche of data entry—obviously a broad task that can apply to many areas of your business. In this regard, virtual assistants can enter data into online platforms such as content management systems, customer relationship management software (CRMs), or e-commerce sites. This helps businesses maintain accurate and up-to-date information across different digital channels.

- **Data Analysis Support:** Virtual assistants can prepare datasets, perform basic statistical calculations, or generate reports based on predefined criteria, assisting you in gaining valuable insights from data.

Document Preparation

Your virtual assistant is there for you in the clutch when you need help preparing documents such as reports, presentations, and proposals. They can also assist with formatting, proofreading, and editing documents.

- **Writing Reports and Proposals:** A virtual assistant can help businesses write reports and proposals by conducting research, organizing information, and presenting it in a clear and concise manner. They can also assist in creating professional-looking reports and proposals by formatting them appropriately and adding visual aids such as charts and graphs.

- **Drafting Emails and Letters**: Hire well, and your virtual assistant can draft emails and letters for you. Take comfort that they will be well-written and reflect your company's tone and style. They can also help you save time by creating email templates for frequently used messages.

- **Formatting Documents**: Uniform documents are important; they tell your clients you are a professional and can be trusted. Virtual assistants can format documents such as contracts, agreements, and policies. In their hands, your paperwork is properly structured and will meet required standards. Virtual assistants can also add tables and headers, and footers to make documents more organized and easier to navigate.

- **Editing and Proofreading**: Ready for an editor? Your virtual assistant can help you edit and proofread documents, so they are error-free and well-written. They can also suggest improvements to the content and structure. Besides, who doesn't want another set of eyes?

- **Creating Presentations**: A competent VA can create professional-looking presentations for businesses by using software such as PowerPoint or Keynote. They can also add visual aids such as images, charts, and videos to make presentations more informative and credible.

- **Converting Documents**: In this modern age, we need to be proficient in many areas. Virtual assistants can convert documents from one format to another, like converting PDF files to Word documents, for instance. This can be useful for businesses that need to edit or reuse documents in different formats.

- **Managing Document Storage**: If you're like me, you can't stand managing document storage. It seems like we carve out time to do it, only to have to turn around and do it all over again! Your VA can help you manage document storage by organizing files and properly labeling and storing them in a secure location. They can also assist in setting up document management systems so files can be easily accessed and retrieved.

Bookkeeping

Managing your business finances can be a huge time suck. The good news is that virtual assistants assist with bookkeeping tasks such as tracking expenses, invoicing, and reconciling accounts. Here are some specifics.

- **Recording Transactions**: If you would rather do anything but dig in and record transactions such as sales, purchases, and expenses, you are in luck. Your virtual assistant can ensure that all transactions are accurately recorded and categorized in the appropriate accounts.

- **Managing Invoices**: Your invoicing process can be better managed when your VA creates invoices, sends them to customers, and follows up on payments. They can also ensure that all invoices are accurately recorded and reconciled with your company's financial records.

- **Reconciling Bank Statements**: Correct record-keeping is the backbone of your business. A virtual assistant reconciles bank statements against your company's financial records to ensure that all transactions are recorded properly. They can also identify discrepancies and resolve them quickly.

- **Generating Financial Reports**: Financial reports such as balance sheets and income and cash flow statements can be generated by your virtual assistant. They can also analyze reports to identify trends or areas for improvement—as they provide insights into your business.

- **Preparing Payroll**: A virtual assistant can prepare payroll by calculating employee wages, taxes, and deductions. They can ensure that all payroll records are recorded to the penny and reconciled.

- **Monitoring Expenses**: Wouldn't you love to know where costs can be reduced? Well, your virtual assistant can do that as they are monitoring expenses. They can also provide recommendations for managing costs.

- **Managing Inventory**: Tracking stock levels, ordering prod-ucts, and reconciling inventory records with the company's financial records are in your virtual assistant's wheelhouse. In addition, they'll recommend how to optimize your inventory management.

Research

Conducting research is an essential component of making smart deci-sions in business. Virtual assistants can assist with conducting research on various topics, such as market trends, competitors, and industry insights.

They are a superior option for research projects due to their efficiency, multitasking capabilities, accuracy, availability, cost-effectiveness, lan-guage proficiency, and organizational skills. They can swiftly gather and organize information, handle multiple tasks at once, provide accu-rate and reliable data, work around the clock (when you have multiple virtual assistants), and save you the cost of hiring full-time researchers. They are trained to overcome language barriers and assist with organi-zation and documentation.

More on how virtual assistants can make your life easier when it comes to research:

- **Performing Market Research**: Every business needs to con-duct market research to help understand its target audience, competitors, and industry trends. This research can include gathering data on customer demographics, buying habits, and preferences. Virtual assistants can also analyze industry reports and trends to identify opportunities and potential threats.

- **Researching Competitors**: You have to stay one step ahead in the game if you're going to last in business. Your VA can conduct research on competitors to give you a greater under-standing of your strengths and weaknesses. They might gath-er data on pricing strategies and provide product offerings and marketing tactics. They can also identify gaps in the market that your business can capitalize on.

- **Researching Products**: If your business is product-oriented, a skillful VA can conduct product research to help you develop new products or improve existing ones. This research can include gathering data on consumer preferences, product features, and pricing strategies. Virtual assistants can also identify potential suppliers and manufacturers.

- **Conducting Industry Research**: Get ready to be up to date all the time! Your virtual assistant can research industry trends and developments to keep your business on top of the latest technologies and best practices. This research can include gathering data on emerging technologies, regulations, and industry standards.

- **Data Analysis**: Large data sets help businesses identify patterns and insights. Now, your VA can do that for you. They'll use tools like Excel and Google Sheets to create charts, graphs, and other visualizations to make the results more comprehensive.

- **Social Media Research**: Every business needs to be on social media. Period. Maybe that's not your jam? Worry no longer! A virtual assistant can research social media trends and engagement to give you facts about your audience's preferences and behavior. This research can include analyzing social media data, identifying influencers, and tracking social media mentions and sentiments.

Project Management

Project management is its own massive animal; if you are a visionary and not so great with details, you may struggle here. Hey, we all need help! Virtual assistants can assist with project management tasks such as creating project plans, tracking progress, and communicating with team members. They can also provide project reports, ensuring that you stay informed about the progress of your projects. You get to stay in your lane, and they stay in theirs!

The following are some areas in project management in which your VA might work.

- **Project Planning:** There are different ways of regarding your projects—either as a high-level overview or you can get specific and fixate on details. A virtual assistant can help businesses with project planning by defining goals, objectives, and timelines. They can also create plans, identify milestones, and establish budgets.

- **Task Management:** Within projects are tasks—and they need to be managed! A virtual assistant can manage project tasks by assigning tasks to team members, setting deadlines, and tracking progress. They can also ensure that tasks are completed on time and within budget.

- **Communication Management:** There are so many moving parts in a large project packed with so many team members. Your virtual assistant can manage project communication by keeping team members informed and up to date on progress. They can also facilitate team meetings and coordinate updates. Now, everyone is on the same page—bye, bye excuses for not getting the work done!

- **Risk Management:** Risk mitigation is a real thing, and many businesses are so busy being reactive that they don't have time to address it. No more! Your virtual assistant can identify and manage project risks by developing risk management plans, analyzing potential risks, and developing contingency plans. They can also monitor risks throughout the project and adjust plans as necessary.

- **Budget Management:** If you or other team members usually blow the budget, a virtual assistant can resolve that for you. They will manage project budgets by tracking expenses, forecasting costs, and reporting on financials. They can also identify areas where costs can be reduced and provide recommendations for managing project costs.

- **Quality Management:** Maintaining quality in your business is a cornerstone of longevity. You don't want to be a flash in the pan. Your virtual assistant can manage project quality by ensuring that deliverables meet quality standards. They can also monitor progress and identify areas of improvement.

- **Stakeholder Management**: Let's not forget the stakeholders, and if you are a busy entrepreneur or business owner, you just might! Your virtual assistant can manage your project stakeholders by analyzing their needs and interests and developing engagement plans for them. They can communicate with stakeholders and provide updates on progress, too.

Sales

Sales make your business go round. We have to spend time here even if we don't have time. If you have been neglecting your sales or trying to fit them in, now, you can do things differently. Hand off sales to your virtual assistant and take back your time! Your virtual assistant can concentrate on this component of business growth. They come to you with specialized skills that allow them to lend a hand in cold calling and sales efforts.

Sales tasks may include:

- **Lead Generation**: Your virtual assistant can generate leads for your business by researching potential clients, qualifying them, and gauging their interest in your business's products or services.

- **Appointment Setting**: Scheduling calls or meetings with potential clients who have shown interest in your business's products or services is no longer your concern. Delegate this to your VA, and enjoy a stress-free life!

- **Cold Calling**: A VA can make cold calls and introduce or pitch your business's products or services to potential clients.

- **Sales Support**: Virtual assistants provide sales support to your business by following up with leads, providing additional information about your products or services, and addressing any questions or concerns potential clients may have.

- **Customer Service**: Providing customer service support to your clients and ensuring their satisfaction with your products or services are jobs your new VA can do in a snap!

- **Sales Reporting**: Your VA can produce sales reports and track and report on sales metrics such as leads generated, appointments set, and sales closed.

- **Sales Training**: A VA doesn't have to stay behind the scenes, either. They can help train your sales staff and share best practices and strategies for successful cold calling and sales.

Appointment Setting

Appointment setting is a critical task businesses need to manage well to grow their customer base. But it's hard to find the time to do it. (Are you sensing a theme here across these tasks? There are so many and no time!) You don't have to add this job to your routine when your virtual assistant can help.

Here's what else they can do in this area that we haven't yet covered:

- **Qualify Leads**: It's so frustrating to spend time on the phone or a video call trying to qualify leads. I'm sure I'm not alone. Your time is better spent elsewhere. Allow your virtual assistant to contact potential clients and qualify them to determine whether they are a good fit for the business. Then they can schedule them to meet with you.

- **Follow Up with Clients**: Let your virtual assistant be the face of your business. They can follow up with clients after appointments to get feedback on your business and schedule future appointments.

Search Engine Optimization

Search engine optimization (SEO) is an essential aspect of any business's digital marketing strategy. SEO involves optimizing a website's content and structure to improve its ranking in search engine results pages (SERPs) and increase organic traffic. But SEO is a many-layered beast if you aren't an expert. All your time can be spent on learning it versus implementing it when a virtual assistant can just jump in and do the optimizing correctly in less time.

These are some of the to-dos involved in SEO:

- **Keyword Research**: Use your virtual assistant to conduct keyword research and identify relevant and high-traffic keywords to optimize your website.

- **On-Page Optimization**: Implementing on-page SEO techniques such as optimizing page titles, meta descriptions, and header tags on your website can all be accomplished by your virtual assistant.

- **Content Creation**: If you're seeking someone to help you generate solid and compelling content that will drive traffic to your page, hire a virtual assistant. They are qualified to create high-quality and relevant content for websites, blog posts, articles, and product descriptions.

- **Link Building**: Link building is a niche job in the SEO realm. A virtual assistant can acquire high-quality backlinks for your business's website, improving its search engine ranking.

- **Local SEO**: Don't forget to optimize your business so it shows up well in local searches. Your virtual assistant can add location-based keywords, optimize your business listing, and build local citations.

- **Technical SEO**: A virtual assistant can perform technical SEO tasks such as optimizing website speed, fixing broken links, and implementing schema markup.

- **Reporting and Analysis:** Regular reporting and analysis of your business's SEO performance, including keyword rankings, organic traffic, and backlinking profiles, can all be managed by your virtual assistant.

Web Design

Designing a website is a long and complex project, especially for businesses lacking the necessary expertise or resources. Plus, it requires specialized skills. Thank goodness for virtual assistants who know what they're doing and can keep you on track!

Here's a more comprehensive breakdown of the tasks involved:

- **Website Planning**: A virtual assistant can help you plan out your website by identifying your business's goals and objectives, defining your target audience, and creating a sitemap.

- **Graphic Design**: A virtual assistant's talents can extend beyond logistics in this area. They can also create custom graphics and designs for your website, including logos, icons, and banners.

- **Website Development**: A highly skilled virtual assistant can build your business's website using custom HTML, CSS, and JavaScript code or website builders such as WordPress, Wix, or Squarespace.

- **Website Maintenance**: With a virtual assistant, you can set up your website and forget it. They will maintain your site by updating content, fixing errors, and ensuring that everything is up to date using the latest security patches and software updates.

- **Website Optimization**: Maintenance is a must to keep your site running well. But you don't have to be bothered with that. Give this job to your virtual assistant and watch them optimize your site for speed, user experience, and SEO by implementing techniques such as image optimization, caching, and responsive design.

- **Website Analytics**: Your site is no good unless its metrics are. A virtual assistant can track the performance of your site using tools such as Google Analytics. They can submit regular reports on website traffic, bounce rates, and user behavior so you can improve user experience.

- **Website Testing**: Occasionally, you will need to test your website to check that it is functioning correctly and is compatible with different web browsers and devices. Yes, your VA can handle that!

Email Marketing

Every business on the face of the planet today likely uses email marketing. It is a pillar of any marketing strategy, permitting companies to connect with their customers and promote their products and services through email campaigns. The downside is that strategizing and implementing these campaigns can take up your time and aggravate you—if you don't know what you're doing. The upside: You can use a virtual assistant in the following ways:

- **Email Campaign Planning**: Every element of your email can be delegated, including email campaign planning. Virtual assistants can help you plan email campaigns by identifying the target audience, creating an email list, and setting campaign objectives.

- **Email Content Creation**: You already know virtual assistants can write—if that's what you want them to do. Turn them loose on email content creation, and they will write your subject lines, body copy, and calls-to-action that are compelling and relevant to your target audience.

- **Email Design**: Creating professional-looking email templates reflecting your brand's identity and aligning with your campaign's objectives has never seen easier with your new VA.

- **Email Campaign Management**: Manage email campaigns by scheduling emails, segmenting email lists, and monitoring campaign performance metrics such as open rates and click-through rates with your VA.

- **A/B Testing**: You need to test the waters of what's working and not with your audience regularly. Your virtual assistant can perform A/B testing on email campaigns by creating multiple versions of the same email and testing different elements in each, such as subject lines, images, and calls-to-action, to determine which version performs better.

- **List Building**: If you want help building your email list by creating lead magnets such as free downloads or offering exclusive content in exchange for email addresses, your VA can accomplish that for you.

- **Email Automation**: Your virtual assistant can set up email automation workflows, like welcome emails, abandoned cart emails, and drip campaigns, to nurture leads and create engagement in the customer journey. When you put your VA to use in this way, you save a ton of money by not hiring an expensive marketing professional—but you still get the job done.

- **Email Analytics**: In short, virtual assistants can handle anything email. But when was the last time you checked your analytics? Be aware of how you're performing with a VA who tracks and analyzes email campaign metrics to identify areas for improvement and optimize future campaigns.

Paid Campaigns

Implementing paid advertising in your business's marketing strategy is non-negotiable. However, creating, managing, and optimizing paid campaigns can be a daunting task, requiring specialized knowledge and skills. Cue your virtual assistant.

Check out some of the ways a virtual assistant can manage paid campaigns for any business.

- **Campaign Planning**: A virtual assistant can help businesses plan their paid campaigns by identifying the target audience, setting campaign objectives, and determining the appropriate budget.

- **Ad Creation**: Delegate your ad creation, such as writing headlines, body copy, and calls-to-action, to your VA, and receive captivating content relevant to your target audience.

- **Ad Design**: A VA can design visually appealing and professional-looking ads, including images and videos that align with your campaign's objectives and brand identity.

- **Campaign Management**: Manage your paid campaigns by setting up ad accounts, creating campaigns, setting budgets, and monitoring campaign performance metrics such as impressions, clicks, and conversions—all with the help of your VA.

- **A/B Testing**: No matter the A/B testing you need done, your VA can handle it—including A/B testing on paid campaigns.

- **Campaign Optimization**: Your campaign won't perform if you don't optimize it. A virtual assistant can do this by analyzing data and making data-driven decisions such as adjusting ad targeting, bidding strategies, and ad creatives to maximize results.

- **Retargeting**: Never lose a customer again with your virtual assistant capable of setting up retargeting campaigns for your website or previous ads.

- **Reporting**: If you've been missing regular reports on campaign performance, including key metrics such as click-through rates, cost-per-click, and return on investment (ROI), it's time to reintegrate these elements. Your new VA can do this for you quickly and easily.

Video Creation/Video Editing

In today's digital age, you must use videos in your marketing, and you need someone who's proficient in editing them for you. From promotional videos to product demos and instructional videos, your videos engage with customers and promote your brand. If you don't have someone to help you, trying to create and edit videos can take you down a rabbit hole of learning skills you don't need to learn. Suddenly, you're out of time on other projects. This isn't optimal. Hire a VA to get you over the finish line.

Virtual assistants can address the following in video creation and editing:

- **Video Planning**: If you need help planning your video content by identifying your target audience, setting video objectives, and determining the appropriate format and style, consider hiring a VA.

- **Scriptwriting**: Specially trained virtual assistants can write scripts for promotional videos, product demos, and instructional videos that will leave your audience wanting more.

- **Video Shooting**: Surprise! Virtual assistants can shoot professional-quality videos using a camera or smartphone. They can optimize lighting, sound, and framing, too.

- **Video Editing**: Hand your virtual assistant raw footage to edit into a polished and engaging video that meets your business needs.

- **Animation**: Certain virtual assistants can also create animations and motion graphics for use in videos. These add visual interest and explain complex concepts.

- **Voice Editing**: If you're not confident about your speaking abilities or don't have the money to hire a voiceover talent— your new virtual assistant to the rescue! They can even edit voiceovers and match the tone and style of the video.

- **Subtitles/Closed Captions**: When your videos call for subtitles or closed captions to make them accessible to a wider audience, call on your VA.

- **Video Optimization**: A virtual assistant can optimize videos for search engines and social media platforms by adding relevant keywords, tags, and descriptions.

- **Video Distribution**: Video distribution is tedious and robs you of the time you need to do other more impactful things. Your VA can distribute videos on various platforms, such as YouTube, Facebook, and Instagram, so they will reach your target audience.

- **Video Analytics**: You must know how your videos are performing, and your virtual assistant can track performance metrics such as views, engagement, and click-through rates. They'll provide reports to help you understand video effectiveness.

Personal Assistance

Virtual assistants are not just for business tasks anymore. This position has expanded to include personal assistance responsibilities, such as scheduling appointments, managing finances, and researching interests. Your virtual assistant can adapt to your needs and preferences, providing personalized assistance and streamlining various aspects of your daily life.

More on what they can do for you personally . . .

- **Schedule Management**: In the olden days of business, you needed an executive assistant *and* a personal assistant, and the two roles never crossed. Now, your virtual assistant can manage your personal schedule, including scheduling appointments, making travel arrangements, and reminding you of important deadlines, so you don't drop the ball on anything.

- **Email Management**: A virtual assistant can manage all your emails, including your personal ones.

- **Event Planning**: We are busier than ever before, and now, you have help to keep all your commitments straight. Your virtual assistant can help plan personal events, such as birthday parties, anniversary celebrations, and holiday gatherings.

- **Travel Planning**: We discussed the benefits of a virtual assistant handling your business travel. That applies to your personal plans, too.

- **Personal Finances**: In addition to managing your business finances, your virtual assistant can pay your personal bills, track expenses, and create budgets.

- **Lifestyle Management:** Your VA can coordinate and supervise household staff, organize personal spaces, and manage personal technology and devices.

After all those long lists, let me just say that pretty much any help you need for your business or personal life can be provided by a VA.

I hope this chapter got your mind going about everything a VA can do for you. I know when I first learned about their potential, I couldn't believe all the time I was going to save. And since I've hired my first VA, my business has changed—because I can focus on growing it—not trying to keep up with it!

Whether you need help with email management, calendar management, travel planning, project management, personal assistance, or another area of life or business, virtual assistants are the answer.

I can help you take that first step to hiring a VA. Reach out to chriskille. com/resources to learn more.

CHAPTER 3

Advantages of Hiring Virtual Assistants

"An hour of planning can save you ten hours of doing."
—Dale Carnegie

Now, you know the nuts and bolts of what virtual assistants can do. You can imagine the immense benefits that come with hiring one for your business. From boosting productivity and saving costs to gaining access to a vast global talent pool, hiring a VA can truly transform your business and help you achieve your goals.

In this chapter, we're going to delve into the incredible advantages of bringing a virtual assistant on board. You'll learn why it's a strategic move that all businesses should seriously consider.

WHAT YOU'LL GET WHEN HIRING A VIRTUAL ASSISTANT

Cost-Effectiveness

Hiring a virtual assistant can be a cost-effective solution for businesses of all sizes due to the aforementioned reduced overhead costs, only paying for the services you need without hiring additional staff, and savings in not paying benefits or taxes.

To be clear, you will need to provide Your VA with tools, but you can use your savings from reduced overhead costs, etc., to set them up with everything they need to get the job done. These tools may include:

- Data security software

- Time tracker

- Payroll system

- Remittance tools

- Secure email system

- Communication tools such as Slack, Trello, etc.

- CRM/Spreadsheets

  When you entrust tasks to a virtual assistant, you sidestep the burdensome costs linked to equipment and software upkeep and upgrades. Now, the only office space and equipment expenses are your own.

Access to a Wide Range of Skills and Expertise

Virtual assistants can provide businesses with access to a wide range of skills and expertise. You benefit from the skills of hand-picked professionals without hiring them as full-time employees.

To reiterate, you will enjoy:

- **Increased Productivity**

- **Flexible Work Arrangements**: Especially beneficial if your workload fluctuates throughout the year. You'll also build relationships with people all over the world, and keep up-to-date on the latest trends and developments in your industry.

- **A Global Talent Pool**

- Scalability

Now, consider these additional benefits . . . .

Reduced Risk

Hiring a virtual assistant can reduce risks. Outsource tasks, and avoid the risk of hiring and training an employee who may not work out in the long term. So much money and time are invested into new employees. If you have to fire them or they leave, you can't recoup this cost. Push your business back from the ledge of potential failure and stop bleeding money. Businesses that use virtual assistants have a much easier time growing.

Skilled Workforce

The Philippines is a beloved hub for outsourcing virtual work. I am continually amazed at the talent we harness at a fraction of the cost of Western countries. And if you have the perception that clients pay their virtual assistants a low wage, let me clear that up. What we pay and what I advise clients to pay virtual assistants is market rate for their cost of living and the country's currency. A virtual assistant's fee or salary in the US is commensurate to the living wage or what is expected and fair for the same position in the Philippines.

The exchange rate between the Philippine Peso (PHP) and major foreign currencies, such as the US Dollar (USD), Euro (EUR), or British Pound (GBP), also works in Western countries' favor.

I would not advocate paying anything less than the recommended rate, so please be aware of the facts surrounding hiring and paying virtual assistants from different countries. If you feel that unfair wages are involved in any transaction, walk away.

Despite all the business I have traded back and forth with the good people of the Philippines, I have yet to visit their country but plan to one day. When I think of how my business has taken off with a large part of its foundation rooted in a country half a world away, I am still shocked. The modern age of business is wild. It is a strange source of pride for me to say I've never been there yet have been able to be a part of such a reciprocal dynamic. I have learned more about this respectful, hard-working culture in the past few years, and I feel incredibly privileged to keep finding out more and to play even a small part in helping their economy.

Filipino virtual assistants are highly skilled and educated professionals with a strong work ethic. You and your business can embrace the advantage of working with such incredible people as you transform your operations and bottom line.

Education

One of the primary advantages of Filipinos as virtual assistants is their education and English proficiency. The Philippines has a literacy rate of 96.6%, with a strong emphasis on English language education.

Technical Skills

Filipinos are also known for their technical skills. They have a high level of proficiency in various computer applications, including Microsoft Office, Google Suite, and other cloud-based software. They are also well-versed in using social media platforms, content management systems, and other digital tools essential for virtual work.

Work Ethic

I've been consistently impressed with the work ethic of Filipino virtual assistants. They are incredibly hard-working, dedicated, and reliable. They constantly go above and beyond to meet deadlines and produce high-quality work.

One of the things that I appreciate most about them is their attention to detail. They take the time to understand the requirements before executing. They are also very good at following instructions. I can assign a complex task, and it will be completed without errors.

English Language Proficiency

The Philippines' high level of English language proficiency is a key factor contributing to the country's reputation as a leading destination for outsourcing virtual assistant services. English is widely spoken and understood, ensuring that communication with clients is smooth and efficient. As English is one of the official languages in the Philippines, it's easy for Filipinos to communicate and work with clients from English-speaking countries. In addition, Filipino virtual assistants are often praised for their neutral accent, which makes their spoken English easily understandable to clients from different regions. Unlike other countries where English is spoken as a second language, Filipinos typically have a clear and accent-neutral pronunciation, eliminating potential language barriers and ensuring comprehension.

Active Listening Skills

Filipinos are known for their strong, active listening skills—essential for understanding instructions and requirements. They pay close attention to details to fully comprehend their tasks. Active listening leads to asking relevant questions, seeking clarification when needed, and proactively addressing any potential misunderstandings.

Politeness and Respect

Politeness and respect have been deeply ingrained in this population from childhood. Virtual assistants are known for their friendly and courteous approach, even in written communication. This deference extends to their interactions with clients, colleagues, and customers. My assistants have been attentive, patient, and accommodating, creating a comfortable and pleasant dynamic that promotes positive working relationships.

Time Zone Advantages

I've been amazed at the time zone advantage of working with virtual assistants in the Philippines. The Philippines is twelve to thirteen hours ahead of my home in Texas—depending on Daylight Savings Time—so when I'm wrapping up my workday, my VA is just starting his. In the evening, I can delegate tasks to him, and they will be completed by the time I wake up the next morning.

It's a huge time saver for me that's allowed me to focus on more strategic tasks. I no longer have to worry about the day-to-day minutiae of my business because I know my VA can handle it. Instead, I work on my agenda: growing my business and developing new ideas.

More benefits of this time zone advantage:

- **Round-the-Clock Productivity**: Welcome to a 24-hour work cycle where tasks and client inquiries are handled quickly, and you stay ahead of your competitors.

- **Reduced Downtime**: Eliminating time-difference challenges means less downtime. What you pay for, you get.

- **Improved Work-Life Balance for Business Owners**: I call this advantage "Taking Back Your Life." Hello, date night, time with the kids, traveling to that country you've always wanted to see. Insert your dream here.

- **Cost Savings**: As tasks are completed continuously, businesses operate more efficiently and avoid unneeded expenses associated with overtime work or hiring additional staff to cover specific hours.

Let's take your business to the next level. Reach out to chriskille.com/resources to learn more.

CHAPTER 4

Challenges of
Working with a VA

"You don't become enormously successful without encountering and overcoming a number of extremely challenging problems."
—Mark Victor Hansen

While there are numerous advantages to hiring Filipino virtual assistants, it wouldn't be responsible of me not to mention the potential challenges that may arise during the hiring process. As is the case when you are hiring for any position, selecting the right virtual assistant requires careful consideration and an understanding of your unique challenges.

One challenge is the time difference. Since the Philippines is roughly twelve hours ahead of the US (depending on your time zone), it can be difficult to coordinate schedules and communicate effectively.

Another challenge is the language barrier. While most Filipino virtual assistants have a good command of English, there may be some communication hurdles, especially if your business deals with technical or complex topics.

Finally, there is the risk of fraud. Some unscrupulous individuals have posed as Filipino virtual assistants to take advantage of businesses. **It** is imperative to do your research and only hire from reputable agencies.

Despite these challenges, hiring Filipino virtual assistants can be a great way to grow your business. You obviously know I am a raving fan! Still, you must be aware of potential obstacles and take the steps to mitigate them.

Now, I want to explore further some of the common hiccups you may face when hiring and offer insights on how to overcome them. Then you can build a successful virtual working relationship. Being aware and implementing proven strategies cultivates a smooth hiring process and maximize your benefits.

Language Barriers:

When interviewing, be ready to face a potential barrier. While English is prolific in the Philippines, there are still variations in English proficiency. Some prospects may have a limited grasp of the language, which can lead to misunderstandings and miscommunications. Remember, these language hurdles can affect clarity in communication and overall productivity. So, tread carefully here.

To mitigate this situation, use clear and concise communication methods. You can provide detailed written instructions to ensure that your virtual assistants understand their tasks and expectations. The use of visual aids, such as diagrams or screenshots, can also help in conveying information. Encourage your virtual assistants to ask questions if they encounter any language-related difficulties to head off any misunderstandings.

Another aspect of the language barrier involves differences in accents and pronunciation. Some Filipino accents may be influenced by regional dialects or local languages. These variations may make understanding verbal instructions difficult, especially during phone or video calls. Both parties must be patient and attentive. Consider using transcription tools or chat logs to make sure everyone is on the same page.

Being aware of language barriers and applying specific communication strategies allows you to communicate more clearly, even when English isn't as proficient. Taking your time to nurture communication leads to better collaboration, understanding, and productivity.

Cultural Differences

Cultural differences can also pose communication issues. Each culture has its own set of norms, values, and practices, which can influence how individuals interpret and respond to instructions. It is essential to be mindful of these cultural differences to avoid misinterpretation of your instructions, which can lead to errors.

- **Misinterpretation of Instructions**: Cultural norms and practices in the Philippines may differ from those in other countries. Virtual assistants may interpret instructions based on their cultural context, which can result in a different understanding from what was intended. For example, there may be differences in the perception of urgency or the level of detail expected in a task. If this is not addressed, it can lead to confusion, delays, or errors in the completion of assignments.

   To avoid this challenge, provide clear and specific instructions; leave no room for assumptions or questions. Virtual assistants should have a complete understanding of the desired outcomes, timelines, and any specific requirements you need fulfilled. Again, it can be helpful to provide examples or visual aids. Encouraging open communication and a supportive environment where people feel comfortable asking for clarification can also alleviate missteps.

- **Communication Style**: Communication styles can vary across cultures, too. For instance, some cultures may have a more direct and explicit communication style, while others may adopt a more indirect approach. Filipino culture tends to be more polite and deferential to authority figures.

These differences in communication styles can lead to misunderstandings or misalignments when you are explaining expectations and goals. If they are not comfortable or feel they are expected to defer to you, virtual assistants may hesitate to ask for clarification or express their opinions.

Establish open lines of communication and create a supportive work environment where people feel comfortable expressing their thoughts and ideas. Assure them their opinions and observations are welcome. Encourage your virtual assistant to ask questions, provide feedback, and actively participate in discussions. Regular check-ins and feedback sessions can bridge the gap in communication styles and ensure that everyone has the same expectations.

TIME ZONE DIFFERENCES

Not surprisingly, when you work with others whose schedules are directly opposite yours, you can expect some challenges. Here are a few:

- **Scheduling Difficulties**: One of the key challenges that you may encounter when working with Filipino virtual assistants is the coordination of schedules across different time zones. The Philippines operates in the Philippine Standard Time (PST) zone, which can be several hours ahead or behind other countries, depending on location. Operating at the opposite end of the spectrum requires excellent communication and trust, especially when it comes to scheduling meetings, setting deadlines, and establishing real-time communication so the work doesn't suffer.

  To address this challenge, use scheduling tools allowing team members to view each other's availability and select meeting times that work for all. These tools consider the time zones of each participant and suggest mutually convenient meeting slots. Make sure to use clear communication protocols here, like providing sufficient notice for meetings and being respectful of each other's working hours. Lead by example to create the culture most beneficial to everyone.

- **Timely Communication Concerns**: Effective communication is the foundation for successful collaboration in a virtual working environment. When team members are located in different time zones, timely communication can be a challenge. Virtual assistants may need to wait for responses or guidance from their counterparts in different time zones, which can slow down progress and stall critical decisions.

To overcome this challenge, Set expectations for response times using official communication channels. From the start, note your preferred methods of communication and share guidelines for how quickly virtual assistants should respond to messages or emails. It may be beneficial to use project management tools or platforms that allow for asynchronous communication, such as leaving messages or comments that can be addressed when the recipient is available.

Employers promote effective communication by encouraging team members to provide regular updates on their progress and detail any challenges. This level of transparency informs all parties of crucial developments—even across different time zones.

- **Impact on Productivity and Collaboration**: Time zone differences can significantly impact the completion of time-sensitive tasks or deadlines. Urgent requests or tasks with strict deadlines will require careful planning and coordination to ensure they are completed on time.

Plan for this and know it is vital to set forth clear and realistic timelines for tasks and projects. Communicate deadlines clearly to virtual assistants, considering their time zone differences. Help your VA feel comfortable communicating proactively with you. Then you will be in the know about potential delays or challenges they may face in meeting deadlines.

- **Reduced Real-Time Collaboration:** Real-time collaboration plays a vital role in problem-solving, brainstorming, and cultivating creativity within a team. Be aware that time zone differences can limit the opportunities for virtual assistants and in-house team members to collaborate, especially during overlapping working hours.

  Again, implement efficient communication tools and practices. Scheduling regular meetings or dedicated time slots for collaboration enables virtual assistants and in-house team members to come together to discuss ideas, share updates, and address any challenges. Also recommended: collaborative project management tools permitting real-time collaboration and document sharing.

  Continually foster a culture of open communication and encourage virtual assistants to reach out for support or clarification. Do this, and you will bring to life a sense of teamwork and collaboration—even in a remote working setup.

QUALITY OF WORK

Many factors can influence a virtual assistant's quality of work. I'll cover them in greater detail below.

- **Varying Skill Levels:** One of the challenges companies may face when hiring Filipino virtual assistants is the potential inconsistency in skill levels. While there are highly skilled and experienced virtual assistants available, others may have a more general skill set. This can affect the quality and efficiency of the work delivered.

  It is important for companies to have a clear understanding of the specific skills and qualifications required for the tasks or projects at hand. Knowing the job requirements and expectations can help in the screening process and in selecting virtual assistants with the skills you need. Conducting thorough interviews, reviewing portfolios or samples of previous work, and seeking references also provide insight into a virtual assistant's skill level and capabilities.

- **Finding Highly Skilled Virtual Assistants**: Identifying virtual assistants with specialized knowledge and advanced skills can be a challenge. You may require virtual assistants with expertise in specific areas such as graphic design, programming, content writing, or digital marketing. But finding candidates with these niche talents may require a thorough screening and assessment process.

  Get in front of this by implementing rigorous recruitment procedures, including conducting skills-based tests or assessments, reviewing work samples, and requesting references from previous clients or employers. Collaborating with reputable virtual assistant agencies or using platforms with a pool of pre-screened and qualified candidates can make finding highly skilled virtual assistants easier.

  Providing detailed instructions, guidelines, and training resources can help bridge any skill gaps and ensure that virtual assistants are equipped with the necessary knowledge and tools to deliver high-quality work. Ongoing feedback and performance evaluations help virtual assistants improve their skills and enhance their performance over time.

  When you carefully define job requirements, conduct thorough assessments, and implement continuous training and feedback mechanisms, you mitigate skill-level inconsistency. This ensures your virtual assistants will possess the necessary skills and knowledge to deliver top-shelf work that meets your expectations and requirements.

- **Lack of Direct Supervision**: Working with a completely remote person means you will need to discuss and agree on how team members will be accountable and work when they are supposed to. Unlike traditional office settings where supervisors can closely monitor and guide employees, remote work arrangements make it difficult to oversee virtual assistants. This can impact the quality, accuracy, and consistency of their work.

- **Monitoring Performance**: Without direct supervision, it can be difficult to monitor the performance of virtual assistants. Employers may not have real-time visibility into the tasks being performed or the progress being made. This can raise concerns about the timely completion of assignments, adherence to quality standards, and overall productivity.

But, like anything else, a little planning goes a long way. From the start, lay out clear expectations and provide detailed instructions to your virtual assistant. Elaborate on project objectives, desired outcomes, and performance metrics. When you do this, your virtual assistant will understand what is expected of them and include a self-assessment of their progress in their routine.

You can also implement regular check-ins and feedback mechanisms to monitor the performance of virtual assistants. Recurring meetings, progress reports, or shared project management tools can help keep track of tasks, so work is progressing as planned. Providing constructive feedback, acknowledging accomplishments, and addressing any performance concerns in a timely manner can help virtual assistants improve their work and maintain high standards.

- **Ensuring Quality Control**: With limited in-person oversight, ensuring quality control can be tricky when working with virtual assistants. You may have concerns about their accuracy, attention to detail, and consistency of work.

Once again, it is important to establish clear quality control processes. This can include implementing thorough review procedures, assigning dedicated quality assurance personnel, or conducting regular audits of work. You can also provide comprehensive guidelines, templates, and style guides to maintain consistency and meet quality standards.

Solid communication channels are crucial for addressing any questions, clarifications, or concerns that virtual assistants may have about their work. Encourage them to seek guidance as you provide a platform for open and transparent communication.

Including clear expectations, detailed instructions, regular check-ins, and quality control processes help maintain the quality and accuracy of the work produced, despite remote arrangements.

Confidentiality and Data Security Concerns

- **Protecting Sensitive Information**: When hiring virtual assistants, plan to protect sensitive information. They often handle confidential data, such as customer information, financial records, or proprietary business strategies, so it is essential to use strong measures to safeguard this information and maintain data security.

  Security concerns may include:

  ○ **Data Security Risks**: Sharing confidential information with virtual assistants introduces potential data security risks. You must be diligent in assessing the security practices and protocols of virtual assistants to eliminate the risk of data breaches or unauthorized access to sensitive information.

    Implement robust security measures. Use secure communication channels and encrypted file-sharing platforms to transmit sensitive information. Ensure that virtual assistants have access to secure work environments, such as password-protected computers and secure internet connections.

    Additionally, confidentiality agreements or non-disclosure agreements (NDAs) can be employed to legally protect sensitive information. These agreements outline the responsibilities and obligations of virtual assistants in maintaining the confidentiality of company data.

  ○ **Data Handling Procedures:** Ensure that virtual assistants follow proper data handling procedures. Use easy-to-understand communication and provide comprehensive training on data security protocols. Don't skimp here!

Communicate security expectations, including the importance of maintaining confidentiality and the consequences of any security breaches. Virtual assistants should be educated about best practices for data protection, such as password management, secure file storage, and regular data backups.

Regularly monitoring and auditing your virtual assistant's data handling practices can help maintain compliance with data security regulations and identify any areas that need improvement. Certain tools and software will track your virtual assistant's access to sensitive information and maintain an audit trail of data activities.

These are the best practices to deploy throughout your virtual assistant's engagement.

LEGAL AND COMPLIANCE ISSUES:

When hiring virtual assistants, companies must navigate potential legal and compliance issues. Adhering to relevant regulations and ensuring compliance with legal requirements will require a little more work on your end, but it will give you peace of mind and head issues off at the path.

- **Compliance with Regulations**: Conduct thorough research to gain a comprehensive understanding of the legal and regulatory landscape you're dealing with, both in your jurisdiction and the jurisdiction where your virtual assistant is located. This includes compliance with data privacy laws, intellectual property rights, employment laws, and tax obligations. Take the time to get to know exactly what you're dealing with.

  Data privacy regulations, such as the European Union's General Data Protection Regulation (GDPR) or the California Consumer Privacy Act (CCPA), may impose specific requirements on the handling of personal data. It is crucial to ensure that virtual assistants are aware of these regulations and that they follow the necessary protocols to protect personal information.

Intellectual property rights must also be considered, especially if virtual assistants have access to proprietary information or contribute to creative works. Always establish ownership and confidentiality provisions through contracts or agreements to safeguard intellectual property.

Employment laws and tax obligations vary across jurisdictions. Companies and *you* need to understand the legal requirements and obligations related to engaging virtual assistants. Ensure compliance with minimum wage laws, tax withholding requirements, and any relevant labor regulations.

- **Contractual Agreements**: To address legal and compliance concerns, establish straightforward contractual agreements with virtual assistants. These agreements should outline the scope of work, payment terms, confidentiality provisions, intellectual property rights, and any other legal requirements specific to the engagement.

It is advisable to consult with legal professionals specializing in labor and employment laws, intellectual property, and data privacy regulations to ensure that all contractual agreements adequately address legal and compliance issues.

Regular reviews and updates of contractual agreements may be necessary to reflect changes in legal requirements or address any specific issues that arise during the engagement.

Do what's recommended, and you can navigate the legal and compliance terms associated with hiring virtual assistants. You'll assure the engagement is conducted in accordance with applicable laws and regulations, lessening any potential legal risks.

Integration with In-House Teams: Virtual assistants and in-house team members must work together to inspire collaboration, communication, and a sense of unity. While virtual assistants work remotely, you must forge a strong connection between them and the in-house teams. Here are some more items to keep in mind.

- **Encouraging Team Participation**: I can't emphasize this point enough. Involving your virtual assistant in team activities and decision-making processes goes a long way toward cementing a trustworthy relationship—in both directions. Provide opportunities for contributing ideas, sharing insight, and making recommendations. This inclusion strengthens team connections and gives a sense of ownership and engagement in the organization's goals.

  Organizing team-building activities, both in-person and virtually, bring teams closer together and improves communication and results. These activities can include virtual social events, team-building exercises, or even occasional meetups. You are building trust, camaraderie, and a shared sense of purpose.

- **Providing Support and Resources:** Supporting virtual assistants with the necessary resources, tools, and information is a must for integration into the in-house team. This includes providing access to relevant documents, training materials, and knowledge repositories. Regular updates and briefings on company news, policies, and procedures keep virtual assistants informed and aligned with your goals.

  You might pair virtual assistants with experienced team members who can provide guidance and support in navigating roles, understanding the company culture, and supporting professional growth.

  This integration fosters collaboration, improves communication, and strengthens unity, leading to higher productivity and a more cohesive work environment.

- **Employee Engagement and Motivation**: Virtual assistants, like any other employees, require engagement and motivation to perform at their best. The remote nature of their work can sometimes lead to feelings of isolation and disconnection. Address this and apply strategies that make your virtual assistant feel a vital part of the team.

  Focus on these initiatives to make sure your virtual assistant understands how important they are to you and the rest of the team.

  - **Addressing Isolation**: To combat feelings of isolation, employers can implement strategies to create a sense of belonging. As mentioned, regular virtual team meetings should be scheduled to encourage interaction.

  - Social engagement activities can also prompt virtual assistants to interact with their colleagues. Consider virtual coffee breaks, online team-building games, or virtual happy hours. These activities provide opportunities for virtual assistants to socialize, build relationships, and feel more connected to the team and the company as a whole.

    Recognize and reward achievements and contributions to boost engagement. Implementing an employee recognition program that acknowledges hard work and celebrates accomplishments can motivate and engage virtual assistants.

  - **Providing Feedback and Development Opportunities**: Feedback and professional development further the growth and motivation of virtual assistants. Please work to provide consistent feedback and development opportunities for the sake of your VA!

    Employers can establish structured performance evaluation processes that include regular check-ins, performance reviews, and constructive feedback. These evaluations help virtual assistants understand their strengths and areas of improvement. They assist in setting goals and tracking their progress. Give specific and actionable feedback focusing on achievements and areas needing development.

Virtual training programs can be offered to sharpen skills and knowledge. Think webinars, online courses, or workshops that address specific areas of professional growth. Giving virtual assistants access to resources and learning materials, such as industry publications or educational platforms, also contributes to their professional development.

Opportunities for career advancement should also take priority to keep virtual assistants motivated and engaged. You can offer new responsibilities, promotions, or special projects that align with their interests and career goals. When you demonstrate commitment to your VA's growth and provide avenues for advancement, they can excel in their roles.

BUILDING/MAINTAINING TEAM CULTURE

Culture is what drives your success or not. You want to dedicate the time and resources to uplifting your team, providing them with clear expectations and resources, and making it known what values are important to you. Even in-person management with other members of your team is easier with remote support.

In particular, pay attention to:

- **How In-House Teams Are Getting Along:** As you know, it can be difficult to create a sense of belonging between virtual assistants and in-house staff. Here are some reasons why this happens and what to do about it:

  - Physical separation and lack of in-person interaction can hinder the development of strong relationships, potentially leading to a perception of isolation and disconnection. Working remotely also contributes to limited opportunities for spontaneous interactions and informal conversations.

- ○ Virtual assistants may feel like outsiders and struggle to interact with established in-house teams due to feelings of intimidation or inadequacy.

- ○ Lack of socialization can impact morale and overall job satisfaction. You are responsible for seeing what's going on and doing your best to resolve it.

Use the tools, resources, and recommended plans discussed to facilitate healthier in-house relationships here, such as providing opportunities for virtual company events, supporting collaboration, and proactively seeking long-lasting solutions.

- **Challenges Incorporating Into Company Culture and Values**:

  - ○ Virtual assistants may have different working styles and communication preferences.

  - ○ Aligning virtual assistants with the company's vision, mission, and values can be a complex task.

- Difficulty with Feedback, Recognition, and Professional Development:

  - ○ Availability and ability to provide feedback may be difficult due to the virtual nature of the work.

  - ○ Recognition and growth opportunities might be less visible or accessible.

- Overcome These Challenges Using the Following:

  - ○ Promote a culture of inclusivity and diversity by emphasizing diverse perspectives and contributions from virtual assistants.

  - ○ Encourage open communication and create a safe space for virtual assistants to express their ideas and concerns.

  - ○ Embrace flexibility and adaptability. Recognize that virtual assistants may have different working styles and schedules.

- ○ Strive to accommodate varying needs and flexibility in work arrangements.

- ○ Continuously evaluate and improve team culture initiatives by seeking feedback from both virtual assistants and in-house team members to identify areas for improvement.

- ○ Regularly reassess team culture initiatives to keep effectiveness and relevance in a dynamic work environment alive.

Building and maintaining a team culture with virtual assistants presents unique challenges, such as integrating with in-house teams and addressing employee engagement and motivation. Practicing strategies that reinforce communication, establish clear expectations, create opportunities for connection and engagement, provide ongoing learning and development, and recognize achievements allow you to meet challenges head-on and create an inclusive team culture.

RELIABILITY AND COMMITMENT

You may face the issue of turnover when hiring virtual assistants. This isn't unique. Many businesses deal with this on some scale. Virtual assistants may transition to different opportunities or have personal circumstances affecting their commitment. To decrease turnover, consider the following tips.

- • **Addressing Turnover**: Focus on creating a positive work environment to improve job satisfaction and employee engagement. This can include providing competitive compensation packages, offering benefits that align with your virtual assistant's needs, and ensuring a healthy work-life balance. When you demonstrate that you value virtual assistants, you empower their commitment and reduce the likelihood of turnover.

  Providing growth opportunities is crucial for retaining virtual assistants. Offering training programs, professional development resources, and pathways for career advancement can motivate virtual assistants to stay with your company. Ongoing support and mentorship with guidance and feedback from experienced professionals can also contribute to your VA's job satisfaction and commitment.

- **Retaining Top Talent**: To retain highly skilled virtual assistants, recognize and reward exceptional performance. Implementing a performance recognition program that acknowledges the achievements and contributions of virtual assistants can be a strong motivator to do a job well. Consider including performance bonuses, special incentives, or issuing public appreciation of their work.

Do the above, and your virtual assistant will feel supported in their professional development, so they will be more likely to stick around and feel connected and engaged.

- **Accountability**: Establishing accountability ensures virtual assistants perform their responsibilities effectively and that they meet deadlines.

These tactics are the building blocks of accountability:

  ○ **Setting Clear Expectations**: Good communication leads to better accountability. Lead the charge and define roles, responsibilities, and performance expectations in detail. Anticipate and answer questions. This includes providing clear guidelines, instructions, and deadlines for tasks and projects. When you follow this protocol, virtual assistants have a clear understanding of what is required of them; they can take ownership of their responsibilities.

  ○ **Regular Communication**: Maintaining open lines of communication promotes accountability. Establish regular check-ins and progress updates to keep tasks on track and do your best to alleviate any challenges or answer any questions promptly. This can be done through video conferences, instant messaging platforms, or project management tools. Regular communication is an opportunity to deliver feedback, offer guidance, and recognize accomplishments—further strengthening accountability.

○ **Performance Monitoring/Evaluation:** Use performance monitoring and evaluation systems to track the progress and quality of work. You may include periodic performance reviews, self-assessments, or peer evaluations. By regularly assessing performance, employers can identify areas of improvement, provide constructive feedback, and address and create a plan to correct any accountability issues.

○ **Collaboration/Teamwork:** Encouraging collaboration and teamwork among virtual assistants bolsters accountability. Through a sense of shared responsibility and promoting collective problem-solving, virtual assistants feel accountable not only to their individual tasks but to the success of the team. Employers can facilitate collaboration through virtual team projects, brainstorming sessions, or regular team meetings.

Setting comprehensive expectations, maintaining regular communication, implementing performance monitoring systems, and fostering collaboration pave the way to accountability. Tasks are completed on time, quality standards are met, and virtual assistants take ownership of their work.

INFRASTRUCTURE AND TECHNICAL ISSUES

• **Internet Connectivity and Power Outages:**

When you are half a world apart from your team members, connectivity glitches and power outages will happen. You must plan for these events with your VA. Infrastructure bugs can disrupt communication and workflow, impacting the productivity and efficiency of virtual assistants. To address them, take the following steps:

○ **Redundancy Measures:** Think about implementing redundancy measures to safeguard uninterrupted internet connectivity. This can include providing backup internet connections (like a secondary internet service provider or mobile data plans) to serve as a resource in case of an outage. Redundancy measures minimize downtime, so your team can continue working.

○ **Backup Power Sources**: Power outages happen more frequently in certain areas, disrupting work schedules and productivity. Employers can provide virtual assistants with backup power sources, such as uninterruptible power supply (UPS) systems or generators, to keep their workstations powered. With these tools, virtual assistants can maintain their work momentum and meet deadlines.

○ **Contingency Plans**: Create contingency plans to address internet connectivity and power outage issues. You might put clear communication protocols in place to inform virtual assistants of any potential disruptions and provide guidance on alternative work arrangements. Develop strategies that will work for everyone, such as adjusting work schedules or temporarily shifting to tasks that do not require an internet connection.

• **Technology and Equipment**: Virtual assistants need access to necessary technology, software, and equipment to maintain their productivity and effectiveness.

○ **Assessing Technological Needs**: Assess the specific technological requirements based on your VA's job responsibilities. Identify the software applications, communication tools, project management platforms, resources, and anything else your VA needs.

○ **Providing Necessary Tools**: Give your assistants access to the tools they need to do their tasks well. You might provide licenses for software applications, grant access to project management platforms, and supply equipment like computers, headsets, and webcams.

○ **Technical Support and Training**: To support virtual assistants in handling technical issues, share resources. You may have an IT help desk or a dedicated tech team. Offer training and guidance on the use of specific software and tools to ensure proficiency.

Addressing infrastructure and technical issues means work meets deadlines. Redundancy measures, backup power sources, contingency plans, and providing necessary technology and equipment are the solutions you need when your VA gets stuck in a tech crunch.

Speaking of stuck . . . let me help you get unstuck. Reach out to chriskille.com/resources to learn more.

CHAPTER 5

Why Are Filipino Virtual Assistants So Popular?

"A professional image is a silent way of speaking."
—Lynn Mikolajczak

Among the various countries known for providing virtual assistant services, the Philippines stands out as the most popular choice. In this chapter, we will explore additional reasons behind the popularity of Filipino virtual assistants and why they are highly sought after in the global market.

The Philippines, an archipelago in Southeast Asia, is known for its warm hospitality, rich traditions, and strong work ethic—making a wonderful addition to your office.

THE MELTING POT OF CULTURES

Filipinos have a natural ability to connect and relate to people from all sorts of backgrounds around the world due to their diverse heritage, adaptability, and open-minded perspective.

Keep these strengths in mind when interviewing and hiring:

Strong Communication Skills

As I have covered, it is amazingly rare to find a Filipino who cannot understand English, resulting in smooth communication across any platform.

Cultural Adaptability

Filipinos are known for their ability to adapt to different situations. Their unique blend of resilience and creativity prepares them to navigate challenges and find innovative solutions. In the virtual assistant industry, clients come from diverse cultural backgrounds; this trait is a significant asset.

TECH-SAVVINESS

The Philippines is one of the top outsourcing destinations in the world, offering a tech-savvy workforce well-versed in virtual collaboration tools and adept at navigating the digital landscape.

WARMTH AND EMPATHY

Filipinos are exceptional at building strong relationships and engendering trust and loyalty. Virtual assistants excel at creating a welcoming and supportive environment, even in remote settings. They want you to feel welcomed and important. Make sure you return the favor!

Over the years, I've been consistently impressed with the Filipino culture. My assistants' skill sets, intense dedication, and work ethic have pushed me to be better—an advantage I did not anticipate.

COST OF BUSINESS OPERATIONS

Aside from labor costs, the overall cost of business operations is lower in the Philippines. Lower rates for office space rentals, utilities, and infrastructures allow virtual assistants to offer their services at more competitive rates.

TIME ZONE COMPATIBILITY

The Philippines is strategically located in a time zone allowing for overlapping working hours with many Western countries. This time zone compatibility is advantageous for both virtual assistants and their clients, as it facilitates real-time communication and collaboration.

IMPROVED INTERNET INFRASTRUCTURE

In recent years, the Philippines has made significant strides in improving its internet infrastructure, making its virtual assistants even more sought after.

The changes and advantages to you are:

Rapid Growth of Internet Penetration

The Philippines has experienced rapid growth in internet penetration in recent years. With the increasing availability of internet service providers, more Filipinos now have access to a stable internet connection, resulting in a larger pool of talented individuals to choose from. And they are just as thrilled to be considered as you are to consider them! I love a win-win situation.

Enhanced Broadband Connectivity

Government and private sector investments have led to significant improvements in broadband connectivity across the Philippines. Fiber-optic networks have been deployed in various cities, offering high-speed and reliable internet, so virtual assistants can better communicate with clients, access cloud-based applications, and perform tasks on time and with the highest degree of productivity possible.

Mobile Internet Accessibility

The Philippines has also seen substantial growth in mobile internet accessibility. With the proliferation of smartphones and affordable data plans, Filipinos can easily connect to the internet, even in remote areas.

Infrastructure Development

New development initiatives have strengthened the internet infrastructure in the Philippines. Recently installed undersea cables have upgraded network infrastructure and expanded data centers. Internet speed has increased, latency has decreased, and stronger bandwidth is available, making jobs requiring substantial data transfer or real-time communication possible.

Reliable Video Conferencing Capabilities

Video conferencing is a requirement in a virtual assistant's job; it is the substitution for working face-to-face. Video collaborations and remote meetings keep the wheel turning and progress ongoing. The improved internet infrastructure in the Philippines has led to more reliable video conferencing capabilities. Virtual assistants can participate in video calls without disruptions, and audio and video quality are now very stable. As a result, clients, colleagues, customers, and you(!) will experience stronger communication and collaboration, regardless of geographical distances.

Cloud Computing and File Sharing

The improved internet infrastructure has facilitated the adoption of cloud computing and file-sharing platforms. Cloud-based applications and services support collaboration, easy file sharing, and real-time updates. Virtual assistants can now access shared documents, work on tasks simultaneously, and provide prompt updates to clients.

Increased Data Transfer Speed

Improved internet infrastructure means increased data transfer speeds, giving virtual assistants the ability and efficiency to handle data-intensive tasks, such as transferring large files, conducting research, or managing data-driven projects. Faster data transfer speeds result in quicker task completion, so multiple assignments can be assigned simultaneously without affecting productivity.

POSITIVE EXPERIENCES AND WORD-OF-MOUTH MARKETING

The virtual assistant industry relies heavily on positive word-of-mouth marketing to build trust and attract new clients. Filipinos have earned a reputation for providing exceptional virtual assistant services, resulting in an extensive network of satisfied clients.

Below are more reasons why people want to work with these incredible people (just in case you're not convinced yet!).

Service-Oriented Mindset

Filipinos are known for their service-oriented mindset and commitment to delivering exceptional customer experiences. Again, this mindset is deeply ingrained in their culture. Providing excellent service is a point of pride. Driven by this value, they go above and beyond to understand and meet the needs of their clients. They want everyone within their orbit to receive personalized and tailored support so they will walk away pleased.

Dedication and Professionalism

Filipino virtual assistants are recognized for their dedication and professionalism. They approach their work with a high level of commitment, taking pride in meeting deadlines and delivering quality outputs. Their professionalism shines through in their communication, adherence to guidelines, and proactive problem-solving. They are a wonderful, reliable asset contributing to a positive working dynamic and increased confidence in clients.

Proactive Problem-Solving

Known for their proactive problem-solving abilities, Filipino virtual assistants approach tasks with a solution-oriented mindset, seeking innovative ways to overcome challenges and provide insights to clients.

Online Reviews and Testimonials

Often, the positive experiences clients have with Filipino virtual assistants translate into positive online reviews and testimonials. These reviews and testimonials are valuable social proof and influence potential clients to choose Filipino virtual assistants for their needs. As prospective clients read about the exceptional experiences of others, they are more likely to trust and engage with these professionals, feeding into even greater popularity.

Ready to get started? Reach out to chriskille.com/resources to learn more.

CHAPTER 6

Misconceptions

"The truth doesn't cost you anything, but a lie could cost you everything."
—Unknown

D espite the popularity of Filipino virtual assistants, there are several misconceptions surrounding them that need to be addressed.

Read on as I debunk these misconceptions and shed light on their true value and capabilities based on my own experiences.

ACCENT

Misconception: Many people believe that Filipino virtual assistants have a heavy accent that will hinder effective communication with clients.

Reality: While it is true that Filipinos have a unique accent influenced by their native languages, their high level of English language exposure alleviates that. English is widely spoken and used as a medium of instruction in schools and workplaces. I haven't had any issues here.

Additionally, they are adept at adjusting their accents to be easily understood by clients. You might consider this a superpower. I do!

WORK ETHIC

Misconception: Some people believe that Filipino virtual assistants do not possess a strong work ethic or the drive to excel in their roles.

Reality: The Filipino culture places great emphasis on hard work, dedication, and a strong sense of responsibility. My virtual assistants take their roles seriously and are committed to delivering high-quality work. They regularly go the extra mile to meet and exceed client expectations.

I've also seen that assistants often have a strong desire to continuously improve their skills and knowledge.

WORK CAPABILITY

Misconception: One of the most common misconceptions about Filipino virtual assistants is that they are limited to performing basic administrative tasks. While it is true that many excel in administrative tasks such as email management, data entry, and scheduling, their skill set extends *way beyond* these responsibilities. (Hopefully, you have read the chapter in the book outlining their far-reaching capabilities. If not, please make sure to check it out.)

Reality: Filipino virtual assistants possess a wide range of skills, including social media management, content writing, graphic design, customer support, and even specialized tasks like SEO optimization and web development. They are highly adaptable and can quickly learn new skills to meet the evolving needs of their clients. I have experienced firsthand how diverse their skills are.

CREATIVITY AND CRITICAL THINKING

Misconception: Another misconception is that Filipino virtual assistants are merely task executors and lack creativity and critical-thinking abilities.

Reality: In truth, Filipino virtual assistants are known for their resourcefulness, adaptability, and problem-solving skills. They offer innovative solutions in many areas for all kinds of businesses. Whether it's developing marketing strategies, creating memorable content, or brainstorming ideas for a new project, they bring fresh perspectives and contribute creatively to their clients' businesses.

MOTIVATED BY LOW WAGES

Misconception: There is a misconception that Filipino virtual assistants are primarily motivated by low wages, and businesses hire them solely because they are affordable. First of all, I have never met anyone who was motivated by low wages. The opposite is usually true.

Reality: While it is true that the cost-effectiveness of Filipino virtual assistants is attractive to many businesses on a budget, we must recognize the motivations outside of monetary compensation. Filipino virtual assistants are driven by their desire for professional growth, learning opportunities, and meaningful work. They take pride in their accomplishments and strive to deliver exceptional results. Investing in their development and recognizing their contributions can lead to increased productivity and loyalty.

Misconceptions surrounding Filipino virtual assistants, such as accent-related challenges, work ethic issues, and a poor grasp of the English language, are unfounded.

Filipinos have a strong commitment to communicate well; they adapt to many different situations, and strive for continuous improvement. Their unique accent, influenced by their native languages, does not impede their ability to communicate clearly.

Their strong work ethic, education, and grasp of the English language, learned in a language-rich environment, make them an easy choice for many of your tasks.

Understanding the realities of Filipino virtual assistants dispels any misconceptions and highlights their value as competent and reliable professionals.

Before you make a decision or develop an opinion, I encourage you to seek out the truth, no matter the topic. Unfounded rumors hurt people at the center of them, and we can always do our best to make sure truths are understood and accepted.

Believing a mistruth is a missed opportunity for you and a perpetuation of a harmful narrative. Learn about the many wonderful qualities of Filipino virtual assistants, and pass on what you know—to the benefit of all.

It's time to see for yourself what a VA can do for you! Reach out to chriskille.com/resources to learn more.

CHAPTER 7

Best Practices

"Practice does not make perfect. Only perfect practice makes perfect."
—Vince Lombardi

A successful relationship with your virtual assistant requires careful planning and implementation.

This chapter explores the best practices of hiring virtual assistants and covers essentials such as having a plan, establishing SOPs, setting KPIs, creating a management plan, determining fair compensation, managing days off and holidays, offering opportunities for advancement, and avoiding common pitfalls.

ENTER YOUR ENGAGEMENT WITH A PLAN

Before hiring a virtual assistant, define your goals, expectations, and the specific tasks you want them to handle. Write a job description outlining the responsibilities, required skills, and qualifications you need. Having a well-defined plan helps you find the right virtual assistant.

Standard Operating Procedures (SOPs)

Establishing SOPs provides a structured framework for your virtual assistant's tasks. Document procedures, processes, and guidelines to ensure consistency and streamline workflow. SOPs help in training, enable efficient task delegation, and a smooth transition in case of personnel changes. Regularly review and update your SOPs to reflect changes in your business.

Key Performance Indicators (KPIs)

Set measurable KPIs to evaluate your virtual assistant's performance. Identify key metrics aligned with their role and responsibilities, such as response time, task completion rate, client satisfaction, or revenue generation. Regularly assess performance against KPIs, too, and provide constructive feedback and support so your virtual assistant can excel.

Management Plan

Devise a thorough management plan to oversee your virtual assistant's work. Schedule regular check-ins, either through video calls or instant messaging, to discuss progress, address concerns, and provide guidance. Implement effective communication channels and collaboration tools to facilitate consistent interactions and keep everyone on the same page.

- **Communication Channels**: Determine the preferred communication channels for collaborating with your virtual assistant. Whether it's email, instant messaging, project management tools, or video conferencing platforms, use the most efficient and reliable methods for regular interaction.

- **Performance Feedback**: Regularly provide feedback on your virtual assistant's performance to lay the building blocks for growth and improvement. Schedule periodic performance evaluations to discuss strengths, areas for improvement, and progress toward achieving KPIs. Constructive feedback advances open communication and a shared understanding of expectations.

Compensation

Determine fair and competitive compensation for your virtual assistant. Consider experience, skills, workload, and market rates. Compensation can be based on an hourly rate, monthly salary, or project rates. Be transparent when discussing compensation and terms, and provide a timely and reliable payment system.

- **Market Rates**: Research market rates for virtual assistant services so your compensation aligns with industry standards. Underpaying may result in difficulty attracting qualified candidates, and overpaying may stress your budget.

- **Task Complexity**: The complexity and skill level required for the tasks assigned should be reflected in the compensation. Consider offering tiered rates for specialized expertise and more complex projects.

- **Days Off and Holidays**: Respect your virtual assistant's need for time off and provide straightforward guidelines for days off and holidays. Consider their local culture and public holidays to accommodate their schedule. Make it known that you welcome open communication to coordinate their workload during absences.

- **Time-Off Policies**: Define policies for requesting time off, including procedures for giving advance notice and coverage arrangements. Foster open communication and flexibility while taking measures to appropriately manage the workload.

- **Holiday Calendar:** Establish a holiday calendar that accounts for your virtual assistant's culture and your business's requirements. Make sure all parties are aware of upcoming holidays and can plan work accordingly.

Opportunity for Advancement

Create a growth-oriented environment by offering opportunities for advancement and professional development. Provide training resources, skill-building opportunities, and clear pathways for career progression. Recognize and reward achievements to motivate your virtual assistant and nurture long-term commitment.

- **Skill Development:** Provide access to training resources, courses, or mentorship programs to help virtual assistants expand their skill sets. Encourage continuous learning and support for their professional development. This will benefit you, too!

- **Increased Responsibilities:** As virtual assistants gain experience and demonstrate proficiency, consider assigning them more challenging and higher-level tasks that align with their capabilities and interests. This will not only keep them engaged and motivated, but it allows them to contribute more to your business.

- **Performance-Based Promotions:** Establish a system for recognizing and rewarding exceptional performance. Implement a merit-based promotion structure acknowledging the achievements and contributions of your virtual assistants.

- **Long-Term Contracts, AKA Security:** Virtual assistants who have proven their value and dedication will feel more secure with long-term commitments and contracts. Providing job security and stability incentivizes them to stay with your organization and invest in its long-term success.

WHAT NOT TO DO

The flipside of advocating for and providing your virtual assistant with the tools to succeed is this rundown of what to avoid.

Before hiring, use caution, and be aware of these common pitfalls.

Not Defining Clear Expectations

One of the most critical mistakes people make when hiring virtual assistants is failing to define expectations from the beginning. Take time to make sure the scope of work, responsibilities, and expected outcomes are well understood. Without a precise understanding of what you need, you may end up with a misalignment of goals and unsatisfactory results.

Skipping the Interview Process

Just because virtual assistants are not physically present doesn't mean you should skip the interview process. Conducting interviews allows you to assess your potential VA's skills, experience, and communication abilities. It also gives you a chance to consider their cultural fit within your organization. Skipping this step can lead to hiring someone who may not meet your expectations or work well with your team.

Overlooking Communication Skills

Don't underestimate the importance of assessing a virtual assistant's communication skills during the hiring process. They need to be able to effectively understand and convey information, respond promptly, and maintain clear and professional communication channels. Poor communication can lead to misunderstandings, delays, and frustration for both parties.

Failing to Provide Proper Training and Guidance

Virtual assistants may require specific training to familiarize themselves with your systems, tools, and processes. Neglecting to provide adequate training and guidance can inhibit their productivity and cause unnecessary errors. Invest time in creating training materials, conducting training sessions, and providing ongoing support.

Ignoring Security Measures

Virtual assistants often handle sensitive information and have access to various systems and accounts. Neglecting to implement proper security measures can put your business at risk. Put impenetrable security protocols in place, including secure communication channels, password management systems, and confidentiality agreements. Protecting your data and maintaining confidentiality should be a top priority.

Micromanaging Instead of Trusting

Micromanaging your virtual assistant can accomplish the opposite of what you want them to do and undermine their autonomy. Remember that you hired them for their skills and expertise, so give them the trust and independence they need to excel. Set clear expectations, establish regular check-ins, and provide feedback, but avoid excessive monitoring or micromanagement.

Failing to Establish Clear Deadlines and Priorities

Without set due dates and priorities, tasks become disorganized, leading to confusion and missed deadlines. Clearly communicate deadlines and priorities for tasks and projects. Utilize project management tools to track progress and keep everyone on the same page. Well-communicated expectations and timelines help virtual assistants manage their workload.

Disregarding Regular Performance Evaluations

Regular performance evaluations assess the progress and effectiveness of your virtual assistants. Failing to conduct timely evaluations can lead to unresolved issues, unaddressed skill gaps, or a misalignment of expectations. Schedule regular check-ins to discuss performance, provide feedback, and identify areas for improvement. These evaluations promote growth, enhance performance, and reinforce a positive working relationship.

Hiring and onboarding virtual assistants can be a transformative experience for your business. But conduct your hiring and management processes the right way.

Avoid these common mistakes, and you will set the stage for a successful long-term relationship as your VA becomes a valuable contributor to you and your company.

Greater success is within reach! Reach out to chriskille.com/resources to learn more.

CONCLUSION

Within these pages, I shared with you the ins and outs of hiring virtual assistants. From understanding the benefits of virtual assistants to developing a strategic hiring process and using the appropriate tools to encourage a successful working relationship, we have covered a wide range of topics to help you navigate the world of virtual assistance.

Hiring virtual assistants offers a multitude of advantages for businesses and individuals alike. Leverage the skills and expertise of your virtual assistant, and you can streamline your operations, increase productivity, and return your focus to high-value tasks.

To get to this place of mutual appreciation and growth, you must approach the hiring process with careful consideration and planning.

To recap, define your needs and objectives before diving into the hiring process. Clarifying the tasks and responsibilities you want your virtual assistant to handle prepares you for a successful partnership. Next, explore various strategies for finding and attracting top talent, including leveraging online platforms, networking, and referrals.

Once you have identified potential candidates, move into the interview process to evaluate skills, experience, and cultural fit. We discussed the importance of conducting thorough interviews and asking targeted questions to evaluate communication abilities, problem-solving skills, and adaptability. Prepare for interviews with these objectives in mind.

You now know the process doesn't end with the hiring decision. Proper onboarding clinches a smooth transition for your virtual assistant as they acclimate to their new role. Emphasize a comprehensive onboarding experience: Offer training on tools and systems, make introductions to team members, share company values, and set expectations right away.

Communication plays a pivotal role in the success of any working relationship, and working with virtual assistants is no exception. Effective communication means establishing clear channels, setting expectations, and maintaining regular check-ins, which will lead to greater collaborations and fewer misunderstandings.

Managing virtual assistants requires a balance of trust and accountability. Your virtual assistant needs autonomy to shine in their role. Giving them this freedom contributes to a healthy work environment and promotes growth as they practice accountability.

Don't forget to think about your virtual assistant's learning opportunities and professional development. Encourage them to sharpen their skills as you offer opportunities for training and advancement. Celebrate their professional wins. Recognizing their contributions leads to job satisfaction and a long-term commitment to your business.

Take a transformative step in your professional journey and hire a virtual assistant.

Finally, remember that hiring virtual assistants is not a one-size-fits-all solution. Practice ongoing evaluations, adjustments, and open communication to further align your virtual assistant's skills with your evolving business needs.

Hiring a virtual assistant is a power move that will catapult you into higher levels of productivity. You may even time-collapse your path to success by years.

So, what are you waiting for?

I'm happy to help when you are ready to hire your own VA. Visit chriskille.com/resources.

ABOUT THE AUTHOR

Chris Kille is a dynamic force across multiple industries. From his headquarters in Frisco, TX, he leads two cutting-edge B2B companies, empowering businesses with streamlined solutions. His reputation for strategizing businesses and entrepreneurships, combined with his expertise, innovation, and ambition, optimize processes, scale capabilities, and maximize profits. He is an outspoken advocate of delegating virtual assistants and embracing efficient payment systems. He feels so strongly about using virtual assistants he even started a placement company to help others take advantage of this business edge. Contact him at chriskille.com/resources to learn more.

DISCLAIMER

While the author has used his best efforts in preparing this book to provide accurate information, he and the publisher make no representations or warranties with respect to the accuracy or completeness of the contents.

The advice and strategies contained herein may not be suitable for your situation and are merely the opinion of the author.

Consult with a professional where appropriate.

The author and publisher specifically disclaim any liability, loss, or risk, whether personal, financial, or otherwise, that is incurred as a direct or indirect consequence from the use and/or application of any contents or material of this book and/or its resources.

The purchaser and/or reader of this publication assumes all responsibility and liability for the use of these materials and information.

Made in United States
Troutdale, OR
11/15/2023

14605417R00060